THE REFERENCE SHELF   VOLUME 42 NUMBER 5

PROBLEMS OF MASS TRANSPORTATION

EDITED BY

DIANA REISCHE

THE H. W. WILSON COMPANY
NEW YORK   1970

THE REFERENCE SHELF

The books in this series contain reprints of articles, excerpts from books, and addresses on current issues and social trends in the United States and other countries. There are six separately bound numbers in each volume, all of which are generally published in the same calendar year. One number is a collection of recent speeches; each of the others is devoted to a single subject and gives background information and discussion from various points of view, concluding with a comprehensive bibliography. Books in the series may be purchased individually or on subscription.

PROBLEMS OF MASS TRANSPORTATION

Copyright © 1970
By The H. W. Wilson Company

International Standard Book Number 0-8242-0413-1
Library of Congress Catalog Card Number 71-140109

PRINTED IN THE UNITED STATES OF AMERICA

PREFACE

You are here and you want to be there. What are your choices for getting there, and how do you select among them —car? bus? trolley? superjet? taxi? monorail? train? The choice will hinge on many variables. How far are you going? Do you own a car? Are you in a hurry? Which method would be most comfortable and convenient? Which can you afford?

Out of millions of such decisions has developed the crisis that now envelops much of mass transportation in the United States. For, when he or she can, the typical American has consistently chosen to drive his car—or if the distance is too great, to fly. Auto transportation and aviation thus suffer from the problems of too much success too quickly attained. Facilities haven't kept pace with demand.

Still serving millions but seldom used by preference, are the other forms of transportation such as buses, trains, subways, trolleys. By definition, mass transportation involves moving great numbers of people from here to there. Ideally it is fast, cheap, reliable, safe, comfortable. Unfortunately, for the majority of Americans who live in the ever-growing metropolitan complexes, transit facilities are inconvenient, uncomfortable, and yet absolutely essential.

Every form of urban transit has its own cluster of crises and petty annoyances. Our magnificent new highways all too often empty into cities with inadequate facilities for the torrent of cars. Subway systems rumble on ancient tracks to the brink of bankruptcy while riders grumble about dirt, delays, rush-hour jams. Buses lumber from traffic light to traffic jam, rarely going exactly where the passenger is heading.

The reasons are complex, but at the nub of the problem is the American's devotion to his car (or his cars). Transit riding plummeted after World War II as America became

3

a car-owning nation. As passengers and revenues dwindled, transit facilities such as trolleys, buses, trains, and subways decayed and were not modernized. Many were abandoned. The downward spiral deepened as deteriorating facilities prompted further riding loss which prompted further drops in service.

Hence, even more people decided to drive. State and Federal governments have poured billions of dollars into crash roadbuilding efforts to provide the roads for this avalanche of cars. But the roads and parking facilities still haven't been built fast enough to stay ahead of demand in crowded metropolitan areas.

Thus, even the most avid highway advocate today has swung to the conviction that cars alone simply can't move the millions in and around the cities every workday. In the crowded cities cars are not the answer for those too poor to own them, too aged to drive them. They are not the answer for the apartment dwellers with nowhere to park them.

Only mass transit can serve such people. Only mass transit can alleviate the traffic snarl. Yet if transit is to be economically viable, it must also lure those who *could* drive if they chose. Present facilities, generally old, generally unpleasant, rarely can lure the rider who has another option.

At the start of the 1970s, however, there are many hopeful signs of a revival in mass transit. The recently created United States Department of Transportation is financing several promising experiments in fast new methods of transit. San Francisco and Washington, D.C., are building highly advanced transit systems that reach beyond each city's borders into surrounding counties. Chicago is revitalizing commuter railroads.

Transit planners are concentrating on linking systems that once competed. For instance, some commuter bus lines are building parking lots at their outlying terminals. Suburbanites drive their cars to the terminal, park, and then ride a bus into the inner city.

Throughout this book, the interrelatedness of the entire transit picture is emphasized. Only air transportation is treated separately.

The book's final section explores the near and far future for mass transportation. Most of the forecasts are somewhat optimistic. Having decided that it *must* have mass transportation, the United States probably *will* have more efficient transit in the future. However, the crystal-ball gazers disagree sharply on what forms this better transit will assume.

The editor wishes to thank the authors and publishers who have generously granted permission to reprint the articles in this volume.

DIANA REISCHE

October 1970

CONTENTS

V. Air Travel: The Problem Is Success

VI. A Look Ahead

I. IS THE SITUATION HOPELESS?

EDITOR'S INTRODUCTION

How gloomy is the mass transit situation? This first section discusses existing mass transit facilities. It sketches the development of U.S. transit and traces the decline that followed World War II.

The articles in this section provide background for all that follows elsewhere in the book. As the final article by Thomas E. Lisco notes, individual choices as to what form of transportation to use depend on the shape of the community, one's pocketbook, and the ease or difficulty of driving and parking. Thus the form the transit picture will take in a specific area depends on dozens of individual local circumstances. The solution that would suit Moline probably wouldn't suit Pittsburgh.

The first article is an overview of urban mass transit, with stress on the need to mesh planning for cars with other forms of transit. The second article, from the *Christian Science Monitor*, offers details of what the transit tangle means for a specific city, Boston. An article from *Congressional Digest* details the scope of existing urban transportation—how many vehicles, what kind, carrying how many passengers how far, and so forth. Next, also from *Congressional Digest*, is an article tracing the development of the present Federal role in transit from the earliest years of the Republic to the present.

An excerpt from President Lyndon B. Johnson's message to Congress urging creation of a Department of Transportation provides a broad survey of past needs and responses as well as present and future realities in transportation. (The Department was established as a Cabinet office on October 15, 1966.) The final selection in this section is an excerpt from an article by Thomas E. Lisco, director of research for the Chicago Area Transportation Study. He ventures an unfashionable opinion: that mass transit today is a veritable Cinderella in our cities, and is on the verge of a transformation from a tattered and frayed servant into a very presentable princess.

URBAN TRANSIT TODAY [1]

In the U.S.A., urban transit—traveling or commuting by train, trolley, bus, subway, or other public transportation—has, for more than a century, been a vital factor in community growth and development. Peacetime transit riding reached a high of nearly 14 billion revenue passengers per year in 1926-28. Under the temporary austerity of World War II when automobile usage was sharply curtailed, transit reached an all-time high of nearly 19 billion passengers in 1945.

The postwar resurgence and expansion of automobile travel, coupled with the shorter work week, more and longer vacations, suburban living, the dispersion of industry, and the advent of television, have taken their toll of transit riders. By 1964, riding had dropped to roughly 50 per cent of its previous peacetime high.

Significant, however, is the marked slowing in the rate of decline, with some transit companies experiencing a reversal of the downward trend. Transit is still doing a big and indispensable job in the morning and evening peak hours to and from central business districts. It remains a basic necessity to the very young and very old, and to those who cannot afford or do not desire to use a private means of conveyance. It is important to millions of motorists who, in many instances, couldn't move through their urban streets in rush hours if transit ceased to exist. It is important to the members of 13 million no-car families, and to 35 million

[1] From "Urban Transit: What's the Situation? Where Is It Heading?" by Walter S. Rainville, Jr., director of research, American Transit Association. *Vital Issues.* 14:1-4. F. '65. Reprinted by permission.

one-car families who have need for transport when the family car is otherwise occupied. It is important to the community at large by enhancing fluidity of movement in congested areas. It brings employees and customers to commercial service, and industrial establishments without requiring parking space. It aids in maintaining downtown and "corridor" real estate values and a stable municipal tax base. . . .

The Automobile Colossus

The automobile is here to stay—at least in the foreseeable future. It has had an impact on every phase of American social and economic life. It has changed the arrangement and mode of living of our cities. The automobile and related industries have assumed a major role in the structure of American prosperity. [More than] 200 million vehicles have been built since 1900. . . .

Small wonder that an earlier Federal Administration should have striven so valiantly and successfully for a multi-billion-dollar national system of interstate and defense highways. No party in power could afford the risk of a Michigan-based national depression simply because there were no roads for cars to run on!

Under the Federal-Aid highway program, in which dollars are matched with the states in the ratio of 90 to 10, jobs are provided for 870,000 workers in roadbuilding and supporting activities; 500,000 more in governmental agencies engaged in planning, designing, supervising, maintaining, and operating the nation's 3.6 million miles of streets and roads.

Inevitable Congestion

The current highway program is unique in its emphasis on urban roads and expressways. Advance planning for local feeder streets and parking facilities has not kept pace with emphasis on the limited access highways themselves. Cities, already congested by the growth in automobile use, are feeling the further impact of the cars brought into the heart of the city by the new expressway systems.

Staunch advocates of the automobile-and-highway as a way of life have reached outspoken agreement with advocates of transit that there is simply not enough space in central business districts to handle the automobiles of all who want to drive into that area. The greater efficiencies of transit in moving persons, and in needing no downtown space for parking, are quite generally acknowledged. Architects and city planners, traffic and civil engineers, are becoming increasingly aware of these relationships, as well as of the fact that—for all its "suburban orientation" of the past several decades—the urban community will retain the central business district as its focus. . . .

A ranking official of the United States Bureau of Public Roads says:

The Federal Government as a matter of policy is for improved transit. . . . Highway officials view transit not as a competitor but as a mode of transport complementary to private transport. [This official considers that] the downtown area is still the most important single destination. Its character is changing, but it will remain the cultural center of the region, center of financial activity, and specialized professional, business, entertainment and similar activities. Because of the concentration of activity, it is the area best served by transit—the largest cities will be heavily dependent on transit, and sometimes rail transit. Most other city trips are almost wholly dependent upon the private automobile or taxi. . . . Highway and transit officials cannot be adversaries. They must be partners. . . .

The "Balanced" Urban Transportation Plan

Writers in the architectural and building fields, as well as in city planning, have given expression to the following thoughts regarding urban transportation planning: it is fast becoming an issue in city survival; transportation problems are enmeshed in the whole urban fabric; cities can't continue to relinquish valuable space to the private automobile; 1980's 100 million nondrivers will require public transportation; preparation of an effective plan for one mode of transportation requires consideration of all modes, conceived of as a system in which the modes are integrated to achieve

complementary and efficient use; that these modes include
walking, the private automobile, the local bus, the express
bus, rail rapid transit, and vertical transportation (eleva-
tors) —each as applied to specified conditions of area density,
distance, and/or travel time. . . .

The transit "riding chart" is characterized by high peaks
of movement twice per weekday, morning and evening, ag-
gregating not more than 4 hours per 24-hour day. The transit operator must, however, have sufficient vehicles available,
with attendant interest, depreciation, and taxes, to meet this
peak passenger movement. Most of these vehicles stand idle,
while their fixed charges go on relentlessly, during the remaining 20 hours of the day, and on Saturdays and Sundays.

The transit manager must also have available, and on
his payroll, operators to drive these vehicles, for whom no
productive work can be found in the off-peak and evening
hours. The transit industry pays a very high wage rate per
actual hour worked because of these daily peaks.

The daily peaks have become sharper with the passage
of time, intensifying the basic economic problems of the
industry.

While these two daily peaks constitute the horns of transit's dilemma from an economic standpoint, they are a boon
to the community in the relief of traffic congestion. Each
passenger included in those peaks is *not* using valuable
downtown space at an average of 75 square feet per passenger in moving, and at 92 square feet per person for parking.
It is for this reason that public officials have come to insist
that every consideration be given to the greater use of improved transit systems. . . .

One thing is certain: because it is a basic necessity of
urban community life, transit will continue to function in
cities large and small—to make physically possible the movement of persons in the larger metropolitan areas, and to
serve the needs of that increasing proportion of the population who will have to rely on public transportation, in even

the smallest communities, because of youth, age, desire, or necessity.

PITY THE POOR COMMUTER [2]

Considering the sorry state of commuter affairs today, the mind boggles at what it might be ten years from now.

In Boston—as in any other major American city—rush-hour travel is for the most part abominably bad. Just ask any commuter. Yet by 1980, what kind of super-tieup might he find himself in?

The 1970s challenge the Boston commuter dilemma in two ways:

The present transportation system must be made to work.

Longer-range solutions for the 1980s . . . must be planned.

Some Boston transportation experts predict the situation will get considerably gloomier before the light begins to dawn on commuters' horizons.

Other experts see gradual progress leading to smooth flowing rush-hour traffic by the middle of this decade.

But all agree that commuters will see significant improvements during this decade. They just suggest different routes to the same goal.

Why is the big-city commuter problem so severe? The answer: Too many cars at rush hour. (Ninety per cent of all intercity travel is by car, and 70 per cent of these cars carry commuters at 1.5 per vehicle.)

And more cars are coming.

At the end of the 1960s more than 2.3 million cars clogged Massachusetts highways. The Registry of Motor Vehicles predicts that by 1975 there will be nearly 2.8 million cars in the state.

The problem, according to Registrar Richard E. McLaughlin, is that roadway construction is not keeping pace. He says that each year another 100,000 cars—enough to tie

    [2] From article by Richard W. McManus, staff writer. *Christian Science Monitor.* p 5. Mr. 25, '70. Reprinted by permission from *The Christian Science Monitor* © 1970 The Christian Science Publishing Society. All rights reserved.

up 300 miles of roadway—squeeze into the state's traffic stream. Yet, he says, the state is able to add each year only 85 to 125 miles of new highways. The Massachusetts Department of Public Works (DPW)—with "concrete" plans stretching to 1990—had wanted to speed the road-building pace.

But in February [1970] Governor Francis W. Sargent suspended, pending further study, most major highway construction inside the Route 128 circle. At the same time he proposed ways to free state and Federal money to greatly improve public transit. Whether this will mark a turning point for weary commuters remains to be seen later in the decade. In the meantime, commuters continue to inch and squeeze into Boston.

By 1975 the population of the Boston SMSA (Standard Metropolitan Statistical Area) is expected to grow from 2.6 million (the 1965 count) to 2.8 million.

Some urban specialists maintain that the suburbs around Boston and other major cities are developing commerce on their own to the extent that home-to-work trip patterns will change in the mid-eighties. These trips, they say, will go from suburb to suburb, while the core city's economic life— and commuter problems—fade.

But over the short range at least—during the present decade—Boston will remain the hub of the region's commercial activities. And the major arteries into the city—the spokes of the region's transportation wheel—will continue to pour traffic daily into the city.

The problems inherited from the past are enormous. The American Automobile Association (AAA) estimates that more than a million motorists drive in and out of the city each weekday. But with only 54,000 on-and-off street parking spaces presently available in the city, the parking situation there has reached near-crisis proportions.

Double- and sometimes even triple-parked cars clog the streets and often reduce the traffic flow to a trickle. Parked cars block intersections of narrow streets; they block access to hydrants. Parked cars hug the curb along streets dotted with "no parking" signs. Cars fill streets beside schools and colleges; they huddle in front of theatres and bus depots.

With so many violations of traffic laws occurring daily, it is questionable whether the present police force could possibly keep up with the pace of violations. As it is, enforcement of parking regulations is sporadic at best.

Cars cause 60 per cent of Boston's air pollution; they raise its dust and they raise the noise level to a roar. (After a heavy snowstorm, just for contrast, walk down a Boston street and hear how quiet it is.)

The Eastern Massachusetts Regional Planning Project (EMRPP), in its 1969 highway and transit master plan, stated the problem this way:

> Until recently, there has been little concern with the design of complete urban transportation systems, although . . . all people and institutions in a metropolitan region are parts of one large community.
>
> Transportation networks have not been planned as large systems like electric, telephone, or water services.

The EMRPP's plans were long-range, but the problems are immediate—coming to work this morning, going home tonight. In the view of Boston Mayor Kevin H. White, the answer is a regional council of governments. This council would bring the Massachusetts Bay Transportation Authority (MBTA), Metropolitan District Commission (MDC), and the Massachusetts Port Authority (MPA) under the control of 104 cities and towns.

Individually, these and other agencies whose function is to provide transportation services, seem incapable of raising their vision to embrace all transportation elements in the metropolitan Boston area and organize them into a coherent, efficient system.

Indeed, this may not be their specific task. But the cost of a poorly functioning system, in terms of delays, frustration, and gasoline burned in idling engines, is borne daily by thousands of commuters.

Some Boston transportation experts feel that proper systems management could get the cars moving again, without waiting until 1980 or 1990.

According to urban specialist William E. Griswold of Systems Analysis and Research Corporation in Cambridge, Massachusetts:

"The real challenge is learning to manage the automobile. It is no longer the case that all cars can go all places at all times."

SCOPE OF PRESENT URBAN TRANSPORTATION [3]

Urban mass transit in the United States, including both privately and publicly owned facilities, is regarded most commonly as comprising all urban systems except taxicabs, suburban railroads, sightseeing buses, and school buses. Included are local motor bus lines, electric street railways, elevated and subway lines, interurban electric railways, and trolley coach lines.

Publicly Owned Systems

Over the past decade urban mass transit has been characterized by increasing acquisition of formerly privately owned systems by municipal or metropolitan area transit authorities—an accelerating trend towards public ownership.

At the end of 1968 approximately 10 per cent of the U.S. urban transit systems were publicly owned—some 114 of a total of 1,094 in operation. These systems were responsible, however, for 56 per cent of the total vehicle miles in the industry and for 67 per cent of total operating revenues. In addition, the publicly owned systems accounted for 69 per cent of the total revenue passengers carried and employed 68 per cent of all urban transit workers.

By the end of May 1969 there were publicly owned urban transit systems in 117 U.S. cities, with more than one such

[3] From "Controversy Over Federal Methods of Financing Aid to Urban Transit Systems, Pro & Con." *Congressional Digest*. 48:292. D. '69. Reprinted by permission.

system operating in each of several of the largest cities. Among the American cities in which urban transit is publicly owned are New York, Chicago, Los Angeles, Philadelphia, Detroit, Cleveland, St. Louis, San Francisco, Boston, Dallas, Pittsburgh, San Antonio, San Diego, Seattle, Memphis, Oakland, and Savannah, as well as a number of less populous areas.

Publicly owned systems operated all of the subway and elevated cars in use in the United States as of the end of 1968, 86 per cent of the surface railway cars, 88 per cent of the trolley coaches, and 45 per cent of the motor buses.

Privately Owned Systems

Urban transit systems in the majority of medium-sized and small cities are in the form of stockholder-owned corporations. Additionally, privately owned systems are operated in such major cities as Baltimore, Houston, Washington, D. C., Milwaukee, New Orleans, Buffalo, Cincinnati, Denver, Atlanta, and Minneapolis.

The overwhelming majority of the privately owned systems operate almost exclusively with motor buses, with only a few such systems utilizing trolley coaches or surface railway cars. No private system operates subway or elevated trains.

Of total passenger vehicles owned by urban transit systems, buses predominated—50,000 buses of an industry total of 61,930 vehicles of all types. Second-ranking vehicle owned was the electric railway car, with 10,745 in use (9,390 subway and elevated cars and 1,355 surface cars). Some 1,185 trolley coaches completed the total.

Motor buses also predominated in totals for overall line mileage, accounting in 1968 for 55,986 miles of lines operated (of a total for all types of vehicles of 57,072 miles).

An estimated 8 billion passengers were carried in 1968 by urban mass transit systems: 5.6 billion on motor buses, 2.2 billion on electric railways (1.9 billion on subways and elevated lines, 253 million on surface railways), 152 million on trolley coaches.

Over the past decade the trend in passenger totals has continued the slow decline which has characterized the entire post-World War II era. From a high of 23.3 billion passengers carried by urban transit systems in 1945, the level had declined to 9.5 billion by 1959. In the ensuing decade the decline has continued in every year but one, to a 1968 level of 8.019 billion persons. This dropoff has affected every type of system at a generally similar rate—railways, trolley coaches, and motor buses.

In the five-year period from 1964 to 1968 operating revenues for all of urban transit increased from $1.408 billion in 1964 to $1.578 billion in 1968—a pattern of increase reflecting higher operating expenses and fares rather than (as will be noted above) heavier use. The growth in revenue was similar in railway and motor bus systems; revenues from trolley coach systems, however, declined over this same period from $46.4 million to $35.9 million, a trend reflecting in large measure the continued phasing-out of such systems.

Since World War II the total number of persons employed in urban transit systems has, with few exceptions, shown a steady decline—from 242,000 employees in 1945 to 149,590 in 1968. While total payroll over this period has fluctuated somewhat in response to varying economic conditions, its long-range trend—as for virtually all of U.S. industry—has been sharply upward. Total urban transit payroll in 1945 was $632 million; for 1958, $831 million; for 1968, $1.1 billion. Average annual earnings per employee have reflected this movement: $2,162 in 1945; $5,036 in 1958; $7,727 in 1968.

THE FEDERAL ROLE IN TRANSPORTATION [4]

Federal activity in the planning, financing, and regulation of the nation's transport system dates from the early

[4] From "Controversy Over Federal Methods of Financing Aid to Urban Transit Systems, Pro & Con." *Congressional Digest.* 48:290-1+. D. '69. Reprinted by permission.

years of the republic. Early Federal aid took a variety of forms, representative examples of which include:

Dedication of outside boundaries of each section of land in new states and territories for road purposes

Establishment and improvement of post roads, military roads, territorial roads, and occasionally bridges, beginning in the early nineteenth century and continuing for many years

Dedication of a portion (3 per cent) of the net proceeds from sales of public lands in newly created states for the purpose of laying out public roads and canals (This was particularly true in those states which entered the Union between 1800 and 1820.)

Identification of navigable waterways as public highways to be forever free, prohibition of collection of tolls for the use of any canal or navigation improvement belonging to the United States, placement of buoys in rivers to identify channels, and (beginning in 1824) the improvement of rivers and harbors

Land grants and monetary loans to railroads, as well as the loan of the Army Engineers in the laying out and construction of railroads—particularly over the years from 1840 to 1870

Improvement of the Cumberland Road (also known as the National Pike) from Cumberland, Maryland, to St. Louis, Missouri, between 1806 and 1844 (Historians have pointed out that Federal construction of this road, by seeming to threaten the jealously-guarded prerogatives of the states concerned, caused the states in turn to drive the Federal Government out of roadbuilding and to take over for themselves primary responsibility for the construction of public roads.)

Changing Modes of Transport

In the earlier years of the nineteenth century the Federal Government had frequently provided impetus to the development of canals and river waterways as primary systems of transportation. As these systems gave way to the development of railroads and, within the major metropolitan areas, rail-based mass transit systems, the Federal role was less evident, limited essentially to development of national or interstate, rather than local, facilities. It was not until the coming of the automobile, the motor bus and truck, the airplane, the subway, and increased use of the electric trolley —all developments largely of the early twentieth century— that the trend of a diminishing Federal role in transportation was reversed.

In 1911, for instance, the Federal Government began subsidizing experimental flights for carrying airmail. In 1912 the Congress authorized the first Federal aid for highway construction and improvement and other direct aid has been provided over the ensuing years to the merchant marine, to commercial aviation, and to renovation and expansion of the inland and coastal waterways of the nation. Over this period the most notable Federal effort has been in the area of highway construction.

The Federal Highway Program

Following authorization of the first Federal-Aid program for highways in 1912, Congress in 1916 passed the Federal-Aid Road Act which became, in effect, the basis for all subsequent Federal-Aid highway legislation. The present concept of a federally-aided and -coordinated national highway system, however, was not advanced formally until 1939, when the Bureau of Public Roads of the Department of Commerce described the need for such a system in a report to the Congress. Acting on these recommendations, Congress in 1944 directed the designation of the Interstate System. In 1955 the Congress enacted a ten-year program of aid to the states in the building of a network of interconnecting high-speed highways throughout the nation, and in 1956 construction was launched full-scale. As originally conceived, the National System of Interstate and Defense Highways was designed to connect, as directly as practicable, the principal

metropolitan areas, cities, and industrial centers, crisscross-
ing the United States with an ultimate 41,000 miles of freeways. Additional Federal legislation in 1961 amplified this
program and called for its completion by 1972.

In 1968, the Federal Highway Act of that year added an
additional 1,500 miles of interstate highways to the system,
bringing its total mileage, when completed, to 42,500. Its
present completion date is in the mid-1970s.

The program is a cooperative one, with the Federal
share of 90 per cent of cost paid entirely by highway users.
The Federal tax on motor fuel and certain other highway-
related taxes are placed in a Highway Trust Fund which
provides the money for the Federal-Aid payments to the
states. No revenues from general taxes, such as the income
tax, are used to finance Federal aid for highways. The Congress sets the annual amounts of Federal aid to be made
available to the states, but the law requires that such authorizations be in conformity with the revenues accruing
to the Highway Trust Fund. The individual states provide
the remaining 10 per cent of cost of those portions of the
Interstate System constructed within their boundaries.

Originally, the Interstate System was expected to cost approximately $41 billion. An increase in the authorized mile-
age, however, combined with substantial cost increases experienced in recent years has raised the overall cost of the
Interstate Highways to a level presently estimated at $56.5
billion.

Urban Transportation Assistance

The first attempt to provide Federal financial assistance
for the direct solution of municipal mass transportation
problems occurred in 1961. The Housing Act of 1961 provided authorizations for three programs, largely exploratory
and experimental in nature, pertaining to urban mass transportation.

Urban Planning Assistance: Transportation planning
was included in the program as a part of comprehensive

planning for urban areas. The Housing and Home Finance Administrator was authorized to provide technical assistance to state and local governments and their agencies and instrumentalities undertaking such planning, and to make studies and publish information on related problems. Also authorized were interstate compacts for transportation planning in interstate urban areas (but not for actual operation of interstate mass transit systems).

Demonstration Grants: The second new program provided Federal contract authority for mass transportation demonstration projects. Such projects, for which the Federal grant could cover two thirds of cost, could include the development of data and information of general applicability on reduction of urban transportation needs, the improvement of mass transportation services, and the contribution of such service toward meeting total urban transportation needs at minimum cost. Federal grants could not be used, however, for major long-term capital improvements.

Loan Program: Loans at a low interest rate were authorized for financing the acquisition, construction, reconstruction, and improvement of mass transportation facilities and equipment. Loans could be made to state and local public agencies where such financing was not otherwise available on "reasonable terms." The facilities and equipment acquired with such loans could be operated by the borrowing agency or by private firms or other public agencies under a lease or other approved arrangement.

In order to assure that proposed improvements were in conformance with sound planning, the law required that a program for the development of a comprehensive and coordinated mass transportation system must have existed or have been in the process of development, although such requirements were authorized to be waived where "immediately urgent need" existed.

Urban Mass Transportation Act of 1964

While the Kennedy Administration and, initially, the Johnson Administration were unsuccessful in their efforts to secure passage of a permanent Federal program of mass transportation assistance, the outgoing 87th Congress did enact an extension of the expiring temporary HHFA [Housing and Home Finance Administration] loan program. Then, in its Second Session, the 88th Congress passed the Urban Mass Transportation Act of 1964 (Public Law 88-365). The present basic law in the subject area, its main features are as follows:

Federal Financial Assistance—"The Secretary is authorized to make grants or loans . . . to assist states and local public bodies and agencies . . . in financing the acquisition, construction, reconstruction, and improvement of facilities and equipment for use . . . in mass transportation service in urban areas and in coordinating such service with highway and other transportation in such areas. Eligible facilities and equipment may include land (but not public highways), buses and other rolling stock, and other real estate or personal property needed for an efficient and coordinated mass transportation system.

Long-Range Program—"No Federal financial assistance shall be provided [pursuant to above section] unless the Secretary determines that the facilities and equipment for which the assistance is sought are needed for carrying out a program, meeting criteria established by him, for a unified or officially coordinated urban transportation system as a part of the comprehensively planned development of the urban area, and are necessary for the sound, economic, and desirable development of such area. Such program shall encourage to the maximum extent feasible the participation of private enterprise. . . . The Federal grant for such a project shall not exceed two thirds of the net project cost [that portion of total project cost which cannot be reasonably financed from revenues].

"To finance grants under this Act there is hereby authorized to be appropriated . . . not to exceed $75 million for fiscal year 1965; $150 million for fiscal year 1966; $150 million for each of the fiscal years 1967, 1968, and 1969; and $190 million for fiscal year 1970. [Authorizations for the latter three years were added by subsequent action of Congress.] Any amount so appropriated shall remain available until expended; and any amount authorized but not appropriated for any fiscal year may be appropriated for any succeeding fiscal year. The Secretary is authorized . . . to make advance or progress payments on account of any grant made pursuant to this Act."

Emergency Program—This provision of the law permits Federal financial assistance where there is an urgent need for the preservation or provision of transit facilities and equipment in cases where the unified transportation plan required above is in the process of preparation but has not yet been completed.

Research, Development, and Demonstration Projects— "The Secretary is authorized to undertake research, development, and demonstration projects in all phases of urban mass transportation . . . which he determines will assist in the reduction of urban transportation needs, the improvement of mass transportation service, or the contribution of such services toward meeting total urban transportation needs at minimum cost. He may undertake such projects independently or by contract . . .

"The Secretary may make available to finance projects under this section not to exceed $10 million of the mass transportation grant authorization [provided above], which limit shall be increased to $20 million on July 1, 1965, to $30 million on July 1, 1966, to $40 million on July 1, 1967, and to $56 million on July 1, 1968. On or after July 1, 1969, the Secretary may make available . . . such additional sums out of the grant authorization . . . as he deems appropriate. [Amounts authorized for fiscal years 1968 and later were added by subsequent action of Congress; later amendatory action also required initiation of a project to develop urban transportation systems which will not contribute to air pollution.]

Relocation Requirements and Payments—"No financial assistance shall be extended to any project . . . unless the Secretary determines that an adequate relocation program is being carried on for families displaced by the project and that there are being provided . . . an equal number of decent, safe, and sanitary dwellings available to those displaced families and reasonably accessible to their places of employment. . . . Financial assistance extended to any project . . . may include grants for relocation payments, as herein defined . . . in addition to other financial assistance for the project . . . and no part of the amount of such relocation payments shall be required to be contributed as a local grant."

Other substantive provisions of the law include three additional grant programs: (1) grants to states and local public bodies for planning and designing urban mass transit projects to be included in a unified urban transportation system; (2) grants for managerial training programs under which fellowships may be provided state and local bodies for training professional personnel in the urban transportation field; (3) grants to institutions of higher education to assist in carrying on research in problems of transportation in urban areas.

The Urban Mass Transportation Act of 1964, originally the responsibility of the Housing and Home Finance Agency, and later the United States Department of Housing and Urban Development (HUD), since 1968 has been administered by the United States Department of Transportation. [In September 1970, the House of Representatives approved the first major Federal program in support of urban mass transit. The bill, passed earlier in slightly different form by the Senate, will provide $10 billion over the next twelve years for new and improved bus and subway systems. In the first five years $3.1 billion will be available.—Ed.]

A PRESIDENT SURVEYS TRANSPORTATION [5]

Two centuries ago the American nation came into being. Thirteen sparsely populated colonies, strung out along the Atlantic Seaboard for 1,300 miles, joined their separate wills in a common endeavor.

Three bonds united them.

There was the cultural bond of a single language.

There was the moral bond of a thirst for liberty and democratic government.

There was the physical bond of a few roads and rivers, by which the citizens of the colonies engaged in peaceful commerce.

Two centuries later the language is the same. The thirst for liberty and democracy endures.

The physical bond—that tenuous skein of rough trails and primitive roads—has become a powerful network on which the prosperity and convenience of our society depend.

In a nation that spans a continent, transportation is the web of union.

The Growth of Our Transportation System

It is not necessary to look back to the 1760s to chronicle the astonishing growth of American transportation. Twenty years ago there were 31 million motor vehicles in the United States. Today there are 90 million. By 1975 there will be nearly 120 million.

Twenty years ago there were 1.5 million miles of paved roads and streets in the United States. Today this figure has almost doubled.

Twenty years ago there were 38,000 private and commercial aircraft. Today there are more than 97,000.

Twenty years ago commercial airlines flew 209 million miles. Last year [1965] they flew one billion miles.

[5] Excerpts from message on transportation by President Lyndon B. Johnson to Congress, March 2, 1966. Text from New York *Times*. p 20. Mr. 3, '66.

Twenty-five years ago American transportation moved 619 billion ton-miles of cargo. In 1964, 1.5 trillion ton-miles were moved.

The manufacturing of transportation equipment has kept pace. It has tripled since 1947. Last year $4.5 billion was spent for new transportation plant and equipment.

Transportation is one of America's largest employers. There are:

737,000 railroad employees

270,000 local and interurban workers

230,000 in air transport

Almost a million men and women in motor transport and storage

Together with pipeline and water transportation employees, the total number of men and women who earn their livelihoods by moving people and goods is well over 2.5 million.

The Federal Government supports or regulates almost every means of transportation. Last year alone more than $5 billion in Federal funds were invested in transportation —in highway construction, in river and harbor development, in airway operation and airport construction, in maritime subsidies. The Government owns 1,500 of the nation's 2,500 oceangoing cargo vessels.

Our transportation system—the descendant of the horse-drawn coaches and sailing ships of Colonial times—accounts for one in every six dollars in the American economy. In 1965, that amounted to $120 billion—a sum greater than the gross national product of this nation in 1940.

Shortcomings of Our System

Vital as it is, mammoth and complex as it has become, the American transportation system is not good enough.

It is not good enough when it offers nearly a mile of street or road for every square mile of land—and yet provides no relief from time-consuming, frustrating and wasteful congestion.

It is not good enough when it produces sleek and efficient jet aircraft—and yet cannot move passengers to and from airports in the time it takes those aircraft to fly hundreds of miles.

It is not good enough when it builds superhighways for supercharged automobiles—and yet cannot find a way to prevent 50,000 highway deaths this year.

It is not good enough when public and private investors pour $15 million into a large, high-speed ship—only to watch it remain idle in port for days before it is loaded.

It is not good enough when it lays out new freeways to serve new cities and suburbs—and carelessly scars the irreplaceable countryside.

It is not good enough when it adheres to custom for its own sake—and ignores opportunities to serve our people more economically and efficiently.

It is not good enough if it responds to the needs of an earlier America—and does not help us expand our trade and distribute the fruits of our land throughout the world.

Why We Have Fallen Short

Our transportation system has not emerged from a single drawing board, on which the needs and capacities of our economy were all charted. It could not have done so, for it grew along with the country itself—now restlessly expanding, now consolidating, as opportunity grew bright or dim. Thus, investment and service innovations responded to special needs. Research and development were sporadic, sometimes inconsistent, and largely oriented toward the promotion of a particular means of transportation.

As a result, America today lacks a coordinated transportation system that permits travelers and goods to move conveniently and efficiently from one means of transportation to another, using the best characteristics of each.

Both people and goods are compelled to conform to the system as it is, despite the inconvenience and expense of:

Aging and often obsolete transportation plant and equipment

Networks chiefly designed to serve a rural society

Services long outstripped by our growing economy and population, by changes in land use, by new concepts in industrial plant location, warehousing and distribution

The failure to take full advantage of new technologies developed elsewhere in the economy

Programs and policies which impede private initiative and dull incentives for innovation

The result is waste—of human and economic resources—and of the taxpayer's dollar. . . .

If the growth of our transport industries merely keeps pace with our current national economic growth, the demand for transportation will more than double in the next twenty years.

But even that is too conservative an estimate. Passenger transportation is growing much faster than our gross national product—reflecting the desires of an affluent people with everincreasing incomes.

Private and Public Responsibility

The United States is the only major nation in the world that relies primarily upon privately owned and operated transportation. . . .

But private ownership has been made feasible only by the use of publicly granted authority and the investment of public resources—

By the construction of locks, dams, and channels on our rivers and inland waterways

By the development of a vast highway network

By the construction and operation of airports and airways

By the development of ports and harbors

By direct financial support of the merchant marine

By grants of eminent domain authority

By capital equipment grants and demonstration projects for mass transit

In years past, by grants of public land to assist the railroads

Enlightened government has served as a full partner with private enterprise in meeting America's urgent need for mobility.

That partnership must now be strengthened with all the means that creative federalism can provide. The costs of a transportation paralysis in the years ahead are too severe. The rewards of an efficient system are too great. We cannot afford the luxury of drift—or proceed with "business as usual." . . .

A Department of Transportation

I urge the Congress to establish a Cabinet-level department of transportation. . . .

The department of transportation will:

Coordinate the principal existing programs that promote transportation in America

Bring new technology to a total transportation system, by promoting research and development in cooperation with private industry

Improve safety in every means of transportation

Encourage private enterprise to take full and prompt advantage of new technology opportunities

Encourage high-quality, low cost service to the public

Conduct systems analyses and planning, to strengthen the weakest parts of today's systems

Develop investment criteria and standards, and analytical techniques to assist all levels of government and industry in their transportation investments

Safety

105,000 Americans died in accidents last year [1965].

More than half were killed in transportation, or in recreation accidents related to transportation.

49,000 deaths involved motor vehicles.

1,300 involved aircraft.

1,500 involved ships and boats.

2,300 involved railroads.

Millions of Americans were injured in transportation accidents—the overwhelming majority involving automobiles.

Each means of transportation has developed safety programs of varying effectiveness. Yet we lack a comprehensive program keyed to a total transportation system.

Proven safety techniques in one means have not always been adapted in others.

Last year the highway death toll set a new record. The prediction for this year is that more than 50,000 persons will die on our streets and highways—more than 50,000 useful and promising lives will be lost, and as many families stung by grief.

The toll of Americans killed in this way since the introduction of the automobile is truly unbelievable. It is 1.5 million—more than all the combat deaths suffered in all our wars.

No other necessity of modern life has brought more convenience to the American people—or more tragedy—than the automobile. . . .

Research and Development

Today, the United States ranks as the world's leader in technology.

Despite this—and despite the importance of transportation in the competition for international trade—exclusive of national security and space, the Federal Government spends less than 1 per cent of its total research and development budget for transportation.

Under our system of Government, private enterprise bears the primary responsibility for research and development in the transportation field.

But the Government can help. It can plan and fashion research and development for a total transportation system which is beyond the responsibility or capability of private industry.

Through Government-sponsored research and development we can:

Fully understand the complex relationships among the components of a total transportation system

Provide comprehensive and reliable data for both private and public decisions

Identify areas of transportation which can be exploited by private industry to provide safer and more efficient services to the public

Build the basis for a more efficient use of public resources

Provide the technological base needed to assure adequate domestic and international transportation in times of emergency

Help make significant advances in every phase of transport—in aircraft, in oceangoing ships, in swifter rail service, in safer vehicles

The department of transportation—working with private industry and other Government agencies—will provide a coordinated program of research and development to move the nation toward our transportation goals. The department can help translate scientific discovery into industrial practice.

Supersonic Transport Aircraft

The United States is pre-eminent in the field of aircraft design and manufacture.

We intend to maintain that leadership.

As I said in my State of the Union Message, I am proposing a program to construct and flight test a new 2,000-mile-per-hour supersonic aircraft.

Our supersonic transport must be reliable and safe for the passenger.

It must be profitable for both the airlines and the manufacturers.

Its operating performance must be superior to any comparable aircraft. . . .

We hope to conduct first flight tests of the supersonic transport by 1970, and to introduce it into commercial service by 1974.

Aircraft Noise

The jet age has brought progress and prosperity to our air transportation system. Modern jets can carry passengers and freight across a continent at speeds close to that of sound.

Yet this progress has created special problems of its own. Aircraft noise is a growing source of annoyance and concern to the thousands of citizens who live near many of our large airports. As more of our airports begin to accommodate jets and as the volume of air travel expands, the problem will take on added dimension.

There are no simple or swift solutions. But it is clear that we must embark now on a concerted effort to alleviate the problems of aircraft noise....

Advanced Land Transport

[In 1965] ... Congress took a long step towards advanced land transportation by enacting the high-speed ground transportation research and development program. This program will be continued at the most rapid pace consistent with sound management of the research effort.

Similar vision and imagination can be applied to highway transport.

Segments of the interstate highway network already in operation are the most efficient, productive roads ever built anywhere in the world. Motor vehicles move at higher rates of speed, more safely and in greater number per lane than on conventional roads. Transportation costs are reduced, and less land area is needed for this volume of traffic.

With the network about half completed after ten years, it is apparent that interstate highways, as well as other roads and streets, can become ever more productive and safe.

Accordingly, I am directing the Secretary of Commerce to:

Investigate means for providing guidance and control mechanisms to increase the capacity and improve the safety of our highway network

Conduct research into the means of improving traffic flow—particularly in our cities—so we can make better use of our existing roads and streets

Investigate potential of separate roadways for various classes of vehicles, with emphasis on improving mass transportation service.

Systems Research

Some of our brightest opportunities in research and development lie in the less obvious and often neglected parts of our transportation system.

We spend billions for constructing new highways, but comparatively little for traffic control devices.

We spend millions for fast jet aircraft—but little on the traveler's problem of getting to and from the airport.

We have mounted a sizable Government-industry program to expand exports, yet we allow a mountain of red-tape paperwork to negate our efforts. Worldwide, a total of 810 forms are required to cover all types of cargo imported and exported. In this country alone, as many as forty-three separate forms are used in one export shipment. Eighty separate forms may be needed to process some imports. This is paperwork run wild.

I am directing the Secretaries of Treasury and Commerce and the Attorney General to attack these problems through the use of effective systems research programs. And I have directed them to eliminate immediately every unnecessary element of red tape that inhibits our import and export programs.

Transportation for America

The Founding Fathers rode by stage to Philadelphia to take part in the Constitutional Convention. They could not have anticipated the immense complexity—or the problems —of transportation in our day.

Yet they, too, recognized the vital national interest in commerce between the states. The early Congresses expressed that interest even more directly, by supporting the development of road and waterway systems.

Most important, the Founding Fathers gave us a flexible system of government. Cities, states and the Federal Government can join together—and in many cases work with private enterprise—in partnerships of creative federalism to solve our most complex problems.

For the very size of our transportation requirements— rising step-by-step with the growth of our population and industry—demands that we respond with new institutions, new programs of research, new efforts to make our vehicles safe, as well as swift.

Modern transportation can be the rapid conduit of economic growth—or a bottleneck.

It can bring jobs and loved ones and recreation closer to every family—or it can bring instead sudden and purposeless death.

It can improve every man's standard of living—or multiply the cost of all he buys.

It can be a convenience, a pleasure, the passport to new horizon of the mind and spirit—or it can frustrate and impede and delay.

The choice is ours to make.

We build the cars, the trains, the planes, the ships, the roads and the airports. We can, if we will, plan their safe and efficient use in the decades ahead to improve the quality of life for all Americans.

The program I have outlined in this message is the first step toward that goal.

I urge its prompt enactment by the Congress.

MASS TRANSPORTATION: CINDERELLA
IN OUR CITIES [6]

Urban mass transportation in the United States is in the early stages of a vast transformation, a transformation that will rival the rags-to-riches change visited upon a fairy tale Cinderella.

There is little question about the rags part of the statement. Mass transportation in the United States can aptly and generally be characterized as dirty, run-down, and financially strapped. It is suffering large deficits and has lost more than half its patronage in the last twenty years. The larger the system, the larger the deficit and the more critical the situation; in New York City the deficit on operations alone was over $50 million in fiscal 1968 with 1969 projections of $150 million. Similar statements can be made about commuter railroads. Deficits abound, systems are run-down and dirty, and stepping into a present-day commuter railroad car is often like entering a museum piece of the nineteenth century.

But riches? Oddly, that is also true. One might think that the consistent failure of mass transportation to hold its own over more than two decades indicates its lack of economic rationale, and thus suggests an imminent and appropriate demise. But the fact remains that mass transportation arteries are as important to the well-being of our cities as express highways. Because mass transportation performs a vital economic function, not only for the individuals who use it, but also for the very form and efficiency of the city, it *must* be made to succeed. Further, there are forces now at work that may help ensure this success.

[6] From article by Thomas E. Lisco, director of research, Chicago Area Transportation Study. *Public Interest.* p 52-74. Winter '70. Copyright, National Affairs, Inc., 1969. Reprinted by permission of National Affairs, Inc. and the author.

The Rational Commuter

To understand mass transportation—its problems and possibilities—requires understanding of its most important customer, the commuter.

The typical urban American's conversation about getting to work follows a predictable pattern beginning with a long monologue that indicates exactly how he saves time getting to work. If he drives, he knows all the tricks. He times traffic signals to the second, follows special routes at different times of the day, and he has pinpointed the location of every speed trap. Altogether, he has carefully thought through the task of getting to work in order not to lose a second's time. He has made an exact science of commuting. A second monologue follows this one and it concerns the others on the highways. What a bunch of idiots they are! Why do they insist on congesting "my" road, and, for heaven's sake, why don't they use mass transportation? It is perfectly clear to the speaker that he uses his automobile for good reasons, but the others who drive must be irrational and peculiar. Their only motive for driving surely must be a totally irrational "love affair" with the car.

If our conversationalist happens to go to work by mass transportation, he, too, has worked his trip out to the smallest detail. He knows the minute he must leave home in order to catch his bus or train. He also knows where to stand in order to catch the car that offers the greatest likelihood of finding a seat, or lets him off nearest his exit at the station. Railroad commuters are known to sit in the same seat of the same car each day, and to be highly resentful when ill-informed interlopers take "their" places.

If the auto driver is outraged by the others who use the roads, the train commuter is bewildered by them. How can people choose to fight expressway congestion, to breathe fumes and build up nervous tension, when they could use mass transportation? The commuter rail traveler sits in his train comfortably reading the paper, while drivers are stuck in unmoving lines of cars on the expressway. Because he generally gets to work faster than if he drove, the auto driver's choice seems senseless to him.

In fact, however, both decisions make sense. Commuters are just as careful in choosing their mode of travel as they are in calculating strategy for the interior portion of their trip. Indeed, it would be odd if they decided their mode of travel off-handedly, and then calculated minor maneuvers to the second.

As one might expect, the basic decision between using the automobile or using mass transportation depends on the relative times, relative costs, and relative levels of comfort and convenience offered by the competing travel modes. Generally, rapid transit and commuter railroads are cheaper than automobiles, and permit the use of the family car by other members of the household. On the other hand, automobiles go virtually any place, at any time. They do not require adherence to a schedule.

In two other aspects mass transportation can sometimes be superior, though sometimes inferior, to driving. One is comfort. Because they are modern, clean, and air-conditioned, as well as involving less strain than driving in heavy traffic, some commuter railroads offer more comfort than automobiles. On the other hand, standing in a crowded car for the entire trip on a rapid transit vehicle may make heavy traffic driving a good deal more appealing. Traffic moves slowly, but at least automobile commuters are seated.

Relative travel times can also favor either mass transportation or automobile. For particular destinations—notably those in the downtown areas of large cities—overall mass transportation travel times may compare very favorably with those of automobiles. For travel between outlying areas of cities, however, mass transportation rarely competes with the automobile. Frequently, direct public transportation lines do not exist. In such cases, mass transportation simply does not provide an alternative to driving.

It is the sum of these calculations that dictates the individual's choice. For some, one aspect may be particularly important, while for others, another may carry disproportionate weight. But overall, there is a remarkable consistency in the response to the alternatives presented. Where mass transportation is a good alternative to driving, people use mass transportation. Where it is not, they drive.

Patterns of Choices

Because commuters make consistent and rational decisions on their modes of travel, the patterns of automobile and mass transportation use across cities are clear. Thus, for travel between outlying areas and downtown—where mass transportation is competitive in time and cost with driving—use of transit and commuter rail lines is heavy. In Chicago, for example, fully 87 per cent of the people going to the downtown area during the morning rush period get there by commuter railroad or transit. Of the remaining 13 per cent who drive, about half do so only because they need their cars during the day. In New York, the relative proportions are even more extreme. There is no mystery to this. In Chicago, rush hour driving to and from downtown is difficult, and "Loop" parking costs are high. Mass transit and commuter rail services are both good. In New York, the mass transit and commuter rail services are even more comprehensive than Chicago's and driving at rush hour is impossible. That few people drive is a foregone conclusion.

In cities with less developed downtown areas, lower parking costs, less highway congestion, and smaller transit systems, automobile driving to central areas comprises a much greater proportion of the travel that is directed downtown. The relative costs and benefits favor highways, and commuters respond by driving.

The patterns are very different for travel between areas that are not downtown. The available mass transportation service is usually restricted to buses, which are rarely time competitive with automobiles because they use the same right of way and make stops. In costs, peripheral travel also favors the automobile. Because parking is available and cheap (mostly free) outside of downtown, automobile costs remain near operating costs. These costs are close to those of mass transportation.

The results are clear. Because peripheral travel is more favorable to automobiles than is downtown travel, both in elapsed travel time and in cost, the actual proportion of travel by mass transportation on the periphery is much smaller than that to downtown. In fact, while all segments of the population use mass transportation for downtown travel, peripheral mass transportation mainly serves persons who cannot drive or afford cars, or who have limited access to them.

The Key to Success: Demand

If relative times, costs, and comfort are crucial to commuters, passenger volumes are critical to mass transportation operations. Whether it be rail rapid transit or commuter railroad, mass transportation cannot exist unless it carries a very large number of passengers. The absolute lower limit for economic investment in surface rail routes is about 5,000 passengers a day, while that for a subway is in the vicinity of 40,000.

These lower limits determine directly where transit and commuter rail lines can and cannot be built. They almost automatically rule out successful rail transit in metropolitan areas of less than a million inhabitants. Cities below this threshold-size simply do not have corridors generating enough travel demand to make commuter railroads or rail rapid transit a good investment. However, even in cities with populations well over a million, mass transportation cannot be a substitute for highways or an instant panacea for transportation problems. Even cities as large as Chicago, Philadelphia, San Francisco, and Boston generate enough traffic to support rail transportation lines only in certain corridors. In all of these cities, the only type of rail transportation that can economically survive is the type that serves travel demands from outlying areas to the city center. Demand for other kinds of travel is simply too diffuse to support rail lines. With present-day technology, such demands can economically be served only by highways.

In certain other cities, also well above the 1 million threshold, even such central-area-serving lines are not assured of economic success. In Washington, D.C., with a metropolitan area population of over 2 million persons, laws restricting the heights of downtown buildings have made the central area so diffuse that the possibilities for economically viable rail transportation are greatly limited. Los Angeles is similar. It is difficult even to find a real "downtown" in Los Angeles.

The only city in the United States that has the density to support a general crosshatching of rail transit routes is New York. The travel demands in all directions are so incredible, over a large area, that parallel rail transit lines can exist only blocks away from one another. There is no other city in the United States, however, in which this condition is presently approached or is likely to be approached in the near future.

Supply: A Key to the Shape of a City

The law of threshold demand for rail transportation lines determines where such lines can succeed. This law, however, has an important converse. Just as rapid transit and commuter railroads cannot exist without high trip-making density, so high trip-making density cannot exist without rapid transit and commuter railroads. Cities such as New York and Chicago simply could not support the economic activities of their central areas without rapid transit and commuter railroads.

As before, the reason narrows down to travel volumes. When volumes of travel are high, rail mass transportation lines can do jobs that highways cannot even attempt. Again, consider the actual numbers. In Chicago, during the three-quarter-hour period between 4:45 P.M. and 5:30 P.M., the six rail transit lines and eight commuter railroads carry nearly 120,000 passengers away from the downtown area. Carrying this many persons in the same time by automobile, with typically existing passenger loads per car, would require 70 express highway lanes. Chicago is already thought to be well supplied with express highways, having 29 limited access lanes leading out from downtown. The addition of another 70 would just about blanket the inner city. In New York, the idea of doing the mass transportation job with highways is even more ludicrous. Commuter rail lines and transit carry more than 1.3 million passengers to and from jobs in midtown Manhattan every day. This job just could not be done with automobiles.

The implications of these figures are dramatic. Plainly stated, if a city wishes to have a well-developed and dense downtown area, it must have high-volume transportation lines to serve that area. The downtowns of Detroit and Los Angeles have been hurt for years because those cities have no rail transportation routes serving downtown. Chicago, Boston, Philadelphia, and New York all have such transportation facilities, and all have been experiencing tremendous building booms in their downtown areas during the postwar years. Perhaps the most dramatic indication of the effects of mass transportation facilities is seen in those cities that did not possess a rail transit system, but have recently built one or are presently doing so. In Toronto, an unparalleled building boom along Yonge Street coincided with the construction of the Yonge Street subway line. This one line completely altered the focus of the central area of the city. Previously concentrated around Queen and Yonge, new high-rise developments have sprung up outside the central core at key stations of the subway.

In San Francisco, the construction of the Bay Area Rapid Transit System is causing a similar transformation to take place on Market Street. This street of recently-faded elegance is currently experiencing a resurgence that will shortly make it regain its place as the most successful commercial street in the city. The cause: a rapid transit system that will not even carry its first passenger for another two years.

Montreal is yet another example of the tremendous response of real estate values to improved mass transportation facilities. There, too, the spectacular growth of the downtown area is associated with construction of a new mass transportation system.

All of these examples illustrate the close relation between the shape of the city and the capabilities of its transportation system. Just as early railway lines dictated the locations of city suburbs 150 years ago, the placements of highways and mass transportation lines mold cities today. For the most part, in our larger cities, this means high-volume transportation lines serving the city center and express highways serving the rest of the city as well as the downtown area. In some cases, there are no high-density travel facilities. In those cases the center of the city is badly hurt by that lack. In the case of New York City the whole inner city is so dense that within Manhattan only a small fraction of the transportation job is done by highways. But now, as in the past, the relation between dense travel needs and high-volume travel arteries holds. Cities with high-density cores have transportation systems capable of handling high-density travel. Conversely, cities without high-density travel transportation systems cannot have high-density cores.

There is, then, an economic rationale for an appropriate mix of mass transportation and highway facilities in our large urban areas. It is also evident that commuters make logical, reasonable, and largely predictable choices of transportation modes for accomplishing their various trips. Further, these reasonable choices of travel modes indicate the types of travel needs that should be served by highways and the types that should be served by rapid transit systems and commuter railroads. What has yet to be shown is the reason why, in spite of economic rationality and indeed utter economic necessity, the rapid transit systems and commuter railroads of this country have generally performed so miserably in the postwar years. Presumably, where there is economic necessity, and particularly where there is a natural monopoly, there is money to be made. However, this natural monopoly has conspicuously not made money nor broken even. Why not?

There are a number of reasons that tend to be somewhat different for rapid transit systems than for commuter railroads. Similarities outweigh dissimilarities, however, and the changes that will revolutionize both commuter railroads and transit systems will be remarkably alike.

The Problems of Transit Systems

The crux of the transit problem can be summed up in two words: comfort and price. There is a somewhat peculiar notion held by many that the modern urban American should be delighted to use mass transit—*any* mass transit—simply because it is cheaper than driving. The overwhelming contrary evidence provided by the amount of highway travel in our cities confuses these people who regard such behavior as economically irrational. Further, they blame this "irrationality" for creating the commuting problem.

On the contrary, it is preposterous to expect anyone with reasonable income, attractive home, and air-conditioned office, to submit to rush hour jostling, crowding, and standing in transit cars that combine inadequate heating and non-existent air-conditioning with poor riding characteristics. People willing to pay a high premium for their comfort at home and in the office, will pay just as much for comfort traveling between them. And when they are faced with the choice between being herded like cattle into a rush-hour transit vehicle, or driving a well-engineered, quiet, and comfortable automobile, the decision is an easy one in spite of additional expense. In fact, only exorbitant parking costs and extreme traffic congestion can guarantee the continued voluntary use of run-down and unattractive transit.

The second reason for transit difficulties—and ultimately the more important one—lies in pricing. The pricing policies of our transit systems could hardly be worse. Not only are fares set at levels that virtually guarantee that transit companies will teeter on the edge of bankruptcy, but they are set with little regard for the most elementary principles of economics.

The Price Level

The major pricing problem results from the fact that almost universally *the fares charged on rapid transit systems in the United States are not too high—they are too low*. For political and other reasons, transit fares are consistently maintained at levels below those necessary for economic operation. The results are disastrous. Faced with persistent shortages of cash, the transit companies are simply unable to function properly. They are unable to provide modern equipment; they are unable to maintain structures and roadways; they are unable to provide protection against crime for the passengers on their property; they are unable to support proper research facilities; they are unable to provide good service. In short, they are not able to perform adequately any of the necessary and normal functions of an up-to-date industry operating in a technologically advanced society.

At first glance, placing the blame for this multitude of problems on the level of the transit fare alone seems an unwarranted, and simplistic response to an extremely complex situation. To challenge such a bold statement of causation, one might be tempted to ask some of the following questions:

1. If fares were actually raised to "economic" levels, how high would they be? A dollar for a trip at present costing twenty-five or thirty cents?

2. How can higher fares answer the problems of transit when the usual postwar pattern has been price rises that lead to less patronage, followed by cuts in service that lead to higher prices, etc.? Can this vicious spiral have any end other than the ultimate bankruptcy of the transit company?

3. If prices are raised to "economic" levels, how will it be possible to provide cheap transportation for the poor people who need it most?

4. Finally, isn't transit inherently *uneconomic* because much of the equipment must necessarily lie idle—and not earning revenue—during most of the day?

Each of these questions is reasonable on the surface, but each illustrates one of the common mass transportation myths. Let us consider them in order.

1. *The incredibly high fare myth.* Rapid transit fares must generally be higher—considerably higher than at present—if the transit industry is to provide the type of transportation that a modern society demands. In absolute terms, however, the necessary price rises are not very large.

Suppose a transit company raises the fare from twenty-five to forty cents. For the great majority of individuals, this extra fifteen cents per ride is not very significant. To the transit company, however, such a fare increase may be very important. Even given the usual patronage response to transit fare increases, this 60 per cent price rise should add to total revenue about 40 per cent.

For most transit companies such large revenue increases are particularly important and can represent the difference between chronic cash shortages and enough revenue both to allow good service and to encourage investment capital. . . .

Fares of a dollar for transit? Given their monopoly position, some companies could conceivably charge that fare and make an exorbitant profit. But operating a transit system is just not that expensive except for unusually long trips. Much more modest fares can assure both deficit-free operation for the present and a solid financial base for the future.

2. *The price-patronage-service-spiral myth.* This myth has its roots in the mistaken assignment of a causal relation between two largely independent postwar changes in urban transit. One, a secular change from lower to higher fares; the other, a dramatic decline in the use of certain types of transit, attended by corresponding service reductions.

Although changes in fare levels have had some influence in determining transit use, their role has actually been quite minor. The automobile has been a much more powerful determinant. The great change in the use of mass transportation since World War II was almost entirely the result of the new availability of cheap and convenient automobiles, and of the advent of urban expressways. During World War II, whether convenient or not, mass transportation had to be used because of gasoline rationing. During the decade of the Great Depression, only a small proportion of the population could afford automobiles. Of course, at no time until after the war did more than a very few urban expressways exist. The result was that, after the war, the change in auto ownership that normally would have been spread over several decades, actually took place in little more than one. At the same time, a massive urban expressway building program took place. The overall consequence of this dual development was that suddenly the bulk of the population was provided with a relatively cheap and very convenient means of transportation that it had never before possessed. Correspondingly, the mass transit and commuter rail companies found their role rather abruptly changed from that of providing most urban transportation services, to that of providing only those services that could compete with the automobile.

Where did the changes take place? Not surprisingly, travel *not* directed toward central areas was particularly affected, especially bus transportation. In the decade following World War II, bus use in major metropolitan areas dropped by roughly a third. The drop in transit use took place just exactly where the automobile could best compete.

At the same time, however, rail transit use to and from central areas fell much less. The slow fall in such transit use continued until the early 1960s when the trend changed to what has been a continuing moderate *increase*. Again, the change was what one would expect. Where rapid transit can compete with automobiles, routes on exclusive rights of way providing competitive travel times to areas with high parking costs, the advent of mass automobile transportation has had only a minor effect. Now that almost all people who want automobiles can have them, the normal process of growth in population and travel is reasserting itself in increased rail transit use.

Why have fare changes played only a minor role? Because other criteria influence choices between travel modes. Variables such as parking costs, relative travel times, and comfort of the transit vehicle, usually are more important than the actual transit fare. Parking costs of two dollars a day at a given downtown destination clearly must dwarf the effects of a ten- or fifteen-cent transit fare rise on travel mode choices. . . . Generally, differences in elapsed times between travel modes . . . can vary by twenty minutes, a half hour, or more. The effects of these differences between travel modes minimize those of potential fare changes. Finally, as indicated above, if comfort can have value measured in dollars per trip, then the actual transit fare becomes relatively insignificant. An unpleasant transit ride at a quarter is just as unpleasant at thirty-five cents.

A price-patronage-service-spiral does *not* represent reality in rapid transit. The role that transit plays in serving the transportation needs of a city depends far more on the nature of the city and of the transit system, than on the fare. If transit is comfortable and convenient, people will use it either at an economic fare or at an artificially low one. Otherwise, they will use it only if they have to. But either way, the amount of the fare will have only a marginal effect on the use of the system.

3. *The cheap transit myth: who pays and who benefits?* The cheap transportation myth is the most unfortunate of all the myths associated with mass transit because the policies that come from it have results exactly opposite to those intended. Virtually the only rationale offered for maintaining transit fares below market levels is to provide cheap transportation for poor people. In fact, what we do through

artificially keeping fares low is to cause tremendous under-investment in mass transportation facilities. Because the investment return is low or negative, it is exceedingly difficult to attract investment to mass transportation. The result is not cheap transit, but, for many, no transit at all. . . .

The major effect of low fares is lack of public transportation, but there is another implication of the low-fare theory that is just as perverse. Although most persons favoring cheap transportation for the poor specify not only that it be cheap, but also that it be of high quality, in actuality this turns out not to be the case. Cheap transportation for poor people almost invariably means poor transportation for poor people. In reality the poor are forced to submit to discomfort and bad service, while the rich drive their automobiles. . . .

The final blow to the cheap transit for poor people policy is a standard economic argument. If subsidization of transportation for the poor is an appropriate public policy, then why not do it directly? Why should all persons using transit be subsidized with scarce public resources to help the few who actually need subsidy? Indiscriminate subsidization of all for the benefit of the few is an extremely expensive type of public aid. . . .

By its very nature, mass transportation will always be cheap transportation. Economics dictates that moving people in groups measured in hundreds costs less than moving them in groups of two or three. However, only if we charge for transit what transit costs can we provide cheap and good transportation—for all the people.

4. *The inherent diseconomies myth.* This myth is included so often in discussions of mass transit that it should finally be laid to rest. The argument states that the extreme "peaking" characteristics of transit demand—high demand at rush hour, low demand otherwise—means transit vehicles cannot pay their way. Transit cars cannot work enough hours during the day to make their use economical. Such is the argument.

Does constancy of use really determine value? Are restaurants "inherently diseconomic" because they are busy only at meal times? Are ski resorts poor investments because they are used only for a few months during the year? Clearly, these enterprises can be perfectly good investments. Transit is the same. Whether any of these investments provides a good return on capital depends, not on the evenness of demand, but rather on the relation between the demand for the service and the costs of supplying that demand. In the transit industry there are many places where demand for the service is more than enough to justify providing the supply.

The Price Structure

The pricing problems of transit begin with the overall levels of fares. Unfortunately, they do not end there. Problems of inappropriate internal fare structures plague the industry, compounding the difficulties already caused by artificially low overall prices.

The crux of the internal price-structure problem lies in the single fare system. The majority of our mass transit systems charge the same amount for six blocks or sixteen miles. This is economically inefficient because it automatically requires that short trips subsidize long ones. Because the fare is set near the average cost of providing service both for long and for short trips, the persons making short trips pay more than it costs the transit company to provide the service, while those taking long trips pay less. . . .

Many trips that would be economically worthwhile at a fare approximating the cost of providing the service are frequently not worthwhile at that cost *plus* the price of subsidizing longer trips. For example, a six-block trip on existing service may well be worthwhile at the twenty-five-cent cost of providing that service, but not at the average forty cents per ride cost of operating the entire transit system. Therefore, persons who would potentially use transit for short trips walk or use other modes of transportation. For no good economic reason, short trips are priced both above their cost and above their value to potential transit riders, thus causing losses to all concerned.

While the single fare system causes the transit user to suffer only when contemplating a short trip, the transit company loses on both types of trip. Not only does it lose revenue by overpricing short trips but by underpricing long ones as well. Just as it costs more to provide transportation for long trips than for short ones, that transportation is correspondingly worth more to the persons who wish to use it. Therefore, if transit companies used rational pricing policies, they would charge higher fares for longer trips. Unfortunately, they do not. The transit companies fail to take advantage of the nature of their demand, and in so doing, contribute to their dismal revenue situation. ...

The single-fare system is not an accident. Such a fare system has an advantage—an advantage that transit companies have been loath to lose—ease of collection. Once the single fare is paid, riders require no further surveillance. No tickets are sold, and no checking is necessary to see that the passengers go only a prescribed distance. These savings in simplicity and in ticket-policing manpower can be considerable. ...

Granted this, however, even where the transit companies can easily differentiate fares, they rarely have done so. It is noteworthy that no United States city having both rail and bus transit has a base fare differential of more than a nickel between types of service, even though rail transit service is generally faster than bus and the average trip length is much greater. Base fare differentials and more than nominal transfer charges between buses and rapid transit are obvious places for rationalizing the pricing system. But even this has not been done.

At this point in the era of automation, the problem of expensive labor for collecting fares really becomes academic. The technology for automatic fare collection is now so easily available and relatively so cheap, that there is no need for human fare collection or direct ticket surveillance at either end of the trip. . . .

Mass Transportation: Future in the Present

Altogether, the serious problems of our big city mass transportation systems are soluble. The economic demands for service exist, and with proper attention given to pricing, comfort, etc., the mass transportation industry will begin to do its job in a manner befitting economic enterprise in the latter part of the twentieth century. This holds true for both rapid transit systems and commuter railroads.

In many places, the stirrings of a new mass transportation future are already being seen. In San Francisco, in particular, there is real attention being paid to the things that matter in mass transit. In the Bay Area Rapid Transit District, the new service will be frequent and fast. The cars will be clean, modern, and comfortable with no standees. The fare will vary appropriately according to distance. There will be automatic fare collection machinery. Transit vehicles will be automated. All these features will contribute to making a system that should be a prototype for twentieth century transit.

In other cities, too, the changes are beginning. In Boston, a much larger system is getting out of the planning stages, and the present system is being substantially upgraded through new equipment and long overdue renovation and modernization of stations. In certain stations it is now a pleasure rather than an obscene pain to enter the Boston subway. In Chicago, more transit lines are being built, and the new equipment there is comfortable, smooth riding, and air-conditioned. Cleveland and Philadelphia are also building new lines and buying new equipment. Other cities are in varying stages of designing completely new transit systems. Even New York, the king of transit and of transit problems, is advancing. There, too, new equipment is slowly spreading through the system. Different types of communications for better service and safety are being tested and adopted. New lines are being built. All over, the transformation in transit is beginning to get under way. . . .

The Government in Mass Transportation

There is no question that the Federal Government plays an increasingly large role in furthering the changes in mass transportation. Many of the improvements that show that mass transportation can be good business are financed, in part, by Federal demonstration and other grants. Much of present-day mass transportation research is financed, directly or indirectly by the Federal Government. . . .

The whole mechanization and automation revolution that has transformed vast sectors of our economy has just begun to touch mass transportation. And mass transportation is an ideal place for it. The moving of large numbers of people has enormous potential for being a much more capital intensive business. Typical transit companies now spend about 70 per cent of their budget for labor. This can and should drop dramatically. The returns to investment in mass transportation technology research and development are very high.

Unfortunately, the ability of individual firms to underwrite the necessary expenditures is limited. No mass transportation company alone has the resources to undertake the development and testing of new technologies that individually may or may not work out. Prototypes of new—and often good—systems tend to be very expensive. For this reason, Government intervention through sponsored research and demonstration grants is enlightened and rewarding social policy. . . .

A further point should be considered. There is a substantial amount of casual evidence to support the popular contention that mass transportation management, both transit and commuter rail, is conservative, old-fashioned, and extremely resistant to change. To the extent that this is true, regardless of who is to blame, the infusion of Federal monies into the industry must certainly be a salutary development.

If nothing else, Federal aid to mass transportation will hasten the day when the owners of mass transportation capital realize the economic potential of their property. When this happens, they will no longer believe that the results of poor management can be tolerated, and they will end such management. When that time comes, the transformation of mass transportation will have come of age: the forces causing it will be self-sustaining and irresistible.

II. VILLAIN OF THE PIECE: THE BELOVED AUTOMOBILE

EDITOR'S INTRODUCTION

If it is convenient to do so, most Americans will unhesitatingly drive themselves to work—one man or woman to a car. Therein lies the genesis of our severest transportation problems. In less populated areas, driving to work and shopping by car makes eminently good sense for those who have cars, as most do. In more densely populated areas, however, where the crush of rush-hour driving taxes roads and parking facilities to and beyond their limits, the tangle begins.

With tens of millions of cars on the road, with two- and three-car families not uncommon, the already congested metropolitan areas are overwhelmed by cars. An unprecedented road-building program has been unable to eliminate traffic tie-ups. It is therefore difficult to conclude today that more roads are the only answer to the traffic problem.

The first article in this section describes America's devotion to the auto, and the consequences for mass transit. Boston, with typical older-city transportation problems, is the focus of the next article. In it a transit expert suggests high tolls on cars carrying only one person to reduce congestion. There follows an article from *Newsweek* outlining a new dimension to the traffic problem: stiffening resistance to further highway building within many cities.

Next, an editorial from the New York *Times* raises an argument that will be heard more frequently in the next two years. The Highway Trust Fund, into which flows between $4 and $5 billion for exclusive spending on roads, expires in 1972. The *Times* editorial advocates new legislation permitting some Trust spending to aid mass transit.

The final article in the section, from *U.S. News & World Report*, surveys current proposals for highway and road construction. If both state and Federal expenditures are considered, the total comes to $320 billion. There will be sharp arguments in the coming decade as to whether spending of that dimension on roads alone is the best answer to current transportation needs.

THE UBIQUITOUS AUTO . . .
MAN'S SERVANT OR MASTER? [1]

Question: Which is increasing faster, the U.S. auto population or the U.S. people population?

Answer: The people, but only because they live a lot longer. Human births are running more than 4 million a year. Still, U.S. automakers are delighted to report that in 1964, for the first time, sales of new automobiles in the United States topped the 8 million mark. . . .

Projections, based on all kinds of iffy factors, indicate that both the auto population and the human population will rise by a little more than 40 per cent in the next twenty years. Fortunately for those who love open spaces, automobiles have a high mortality rate—about 5 million are scrapped each year. Average age at which cars are now hitting the junk heap: six years. Even so, the cars are multiplying at a rate that alarms or delights—depending on your viewpoint. In 1941, there were 11.4 cars per mile of road in the United States. Today there are 22 cars for every mile—and that despite vast road-building programs in virtually every state of the union.

For many individuals, *transportation* and *car* are practically synonyms. But for the economy as a whole, and for the nation as a whole, the automobile is but one part of a complex system of moving goods and people.

[1] From article in *Senior Scholastic*. 86:6-9. F. 4, '65. Reprinted by permission of Scholastic Magazines, Inc., from *Senior Scholastic*, © 1965 by Scholastic Magazines, Inc.

Increasingly, experts and amateurs alike are questioning whether adequate planning is going into this vital sector of our society. They ask whether rational decisions are being made about the type of transportation that is best suited—in financial *and* social terms—for each given need.

"Each segment of this vast [transportation] industry . . . has its special problems," commented an article in the *Christian Science Monitor* two years ago [in 1963]. "Most of them center in the question of where the investment capital will come from to take care of the needed modernization of equipment."

In the intervening two years, the situation has remained the same. The cost of the interstate highway system, for instance, is now running about one million dollars to the mile. Within congested areas, it is far higher. The Institute of Public Administration reported . . . [in 1963] that capital expenditures of $9.8 billion would be needed to build rail, bus, and subway transit facilities—just to meet the U.S. needs for the next decade. . . .

It is difficult to think of a product or service that doesn't involve movement of people or goods at least once. On any map, transportation networks—roads, railroads, rivers—tend to resemble nothing so much as arteries and blood vessels. For the nation's economy, they are indeed the life-carrying network.

Whatever its form, transportation on a nationwide scale is a costly business. And whatever its form, the public purse generally supplies some of the underwriting. Because the convenient movement of goods and people is essential to any nation's economic health and to its system of defenses, keeping the transportation system healthy has always been considered in the public interest. Federal money made the vast railroad system possible; Federal money keeps uneconomical airlines flying and uneconomic ships moving. Local money builds roads and pays for their upkeep.

Many of the decisions as to *which* methods of transportation should be emphasized inevitably become, in part, public decisions. They come at every level of government—local, state, Federal—because every level of government is shelling out money for transportation systems.

To give just one example: almost everyone knows the Federal Government is backing the construction of the $41 billion Interstate Highway System, a 41,000 mile border-to-border network of roads that will be free of stoplights or intersections. Most people know, too, that the Federal Government provides 90 per cent of the funds, while the states provide 10 per cent. The assumption often made, therefore, is that the national Government is the big spender on roads. But according to the Federal Bureau of Public Roads, of the estimated 1964 expenditures on *all* public roads and highways—$12.8 billion—only $3.9 billion was Federal money. The other $8.9 billion was spent by state and local governments.

The demand for these new roads is linked partly to the growth of the trucking industry. . . . But more than anything else it is linked to the rapid growth of car ownership. More and more Americans are using automobiles not only as a luxury but as their sole means of getting to and from work. According to the 1960 census, 64 per cent of U.S. workers traveled to and from their jobs in private cars. Only 12 per cent used some kind of public transportation—buses, subways, commuter trains, or the like. (The rest walked, bicycled, taxied, or used some other method.)

The trend to multiple car ownership is growing. Some 11,300,000 families had more than one car in 1963; and 750,000 owned three. Only about 20 per cent of the families in the United States were getting along with zero cars.

For the automobile industry, such statistics are a sheer delight. Only a few years ago auto makers were saying that car sales had hit a plateau, that annual sales would remain at between 6 and 7 million year after year. Now, with an eight-million year behind them—an eight-million year *despite* strikes at Ford and General Motors—they are confidently talking about nine- and ten-million years.

Those additional cars mean additional need for roads, parking places, traffic signals, traffic police, and all the other services necessitated by the automobile. Increasingly, planners are coming to believe that the task of building highways is a never-ending one. Each new highway, they say, generates new traffic: more people take trips they wouldn't have taken before. And each new highway puts new pressure on the roads—and the cities—it feeds into.

More and more often, plans for new freeways into and around cities are encountering fierce local resistance from people whose homes are in the way, or from defenders of parks that are to be crossed. The objections aren't necessarily to *all* freeways—just to freeways in *their* part of town, or through a historic neighborhood or a park. [See "Fighting the Freeway," in this section, below.] . . .

Meanwhile, Federal authorities have taken steps to insure that the communities concerned actually *want* the roads they are getting. After July 1 [1965] no Federal money in excess of $50,000 will be available for highways in urban areas unless the roads fit into comprehensive highway plans that have already won approval of state and local authorities.

That decision by Congress represented a victory for those who have been arguing that it can be harmful to rush ahead with any one transportation system unless all other factors are taken into account. It also brings to the front the long-standing argument between "automobile people" and "mass transit people." Generally, those who argue against the building of further roads to serve the automobile are city dwellers, concerned about urban values. To them the automobile is primarily responsible for the clogging of city streets and for the concrete blight they see snaking its way through their beloved town.

Both anti- and pro-auto people agree on one fact. The average American, given his choice on how to get from point to point, prefers to get into his car at his front door, drive it to the doorway of his destination, and get out. From here on, agreement ends.

The pro-auto people believe that the average American cannot and should not be discouraged from using his preferred means of travel. The anti-auto people believe that he *must* be discouraged in certain circumstances—or else he will eventually discourage himself. As the number of cars on the roads increases, so does the difficulty of finding a parking place or of moving at more than a funereal pace in city streets.

The problem, says C. W. Griffin, Jr., an engineer specializing in city planning, is that the private car has become a symbol of aristocratic superiority to the American. Writing in *Harper's Magazine,* Griffin adds that snobbery also seems to pervade government's attitude toward transportation.

Cities whose mass transit equipment is ready for the museum compete in erecting luxurious air terminals to attract and impress air travelers. At the same time they are alienating their own city-dwelling pedestrians. While mass transit founders, they carve, flatten, and sprawl the cities for freeways and parking lots to attract more automobiles; they herd pedestrians into narrowed sidewalks, exposing them to ever-increasing hazards, noise, and exhaust fumes.

Taking an even harder line, the New York *Times* suggested editorially that what that city ought to be doing is to discourage, by every means available (in other words, make as unpleasant as possible), the presence of the auto in the heart of the city, thus forcing people to fall back on public transportation. With the city streets cleared of private autos, public transportation would be able to move more swiftly.

To such criticisms—and they are widespread—the "auto people" point out that the "sprawl" or dispersion of cities began before the automobile. Furthermore, they argue that the debate over auto versus mass transit is senseless.

Some of these critics seem to have in their minds the ideal of a small, peaceful nineteenth century town, where people walked to and from their jobs and spent their evenings rocking on the front porch [says Lynn A. Townsend, president of Chrysler Corporation]. With this ideal in mind, it is no surprise that they speak of the automobile as a mechanical monster destroying the basic values of our civilization.

The auto has come to stay, say its champions, and it cannot be legislated out of existence.

The "auto people" found . . . [in 1964] that they had an influential patron. Signing a $2.4 billion bill to improve primary and secondary roads, President Johnson declared:

> For much too long the man who owns and drives an automobile has been treated like a stepchild. We require him to pay for the highways he uses and we require him to pay in advance.
> We divert his taxes to other uses but we delay the building of the roads he deserves. We denounce him for getting snarled in traffic jams not of his own making. We complain about what he costs us but we never thank him for what he adds to the worth and wealth of our economy.

The mere production of automobiles is indeed a tremendous factor in the nation's economic vigor. Add to it the peripheral jobs—the service stations, the traffic cops, the road construction crews, the sign painters—and you have a very important factor in the national wealth. Still, in one sense highway users *aren't* paying their own way entirely. Statistics from the Bureau of Public Roads—certainly no foe of the automobile—show that in 1960 the country spent $1.5 billion *more* for building, maintaining, and policing streets and highways than was received from highway users (through tolls, gasoline taxes, etc.).

So the arguments continue. Often the key to the dispute is land, particularly urban land. Where large amounts of space are available—in rural areas, in most suburbs—the private automobile is the only feasible way for people to get about. The arguments heat up when the question involves cities, particularly big cities. In the older cities such as Boston, Philadelphia, New York, New Orleans, San Francisco, where downtown areas are compact and land severely limited, the taking of land for a highway or garage involves the taking away of that land from some other and probably more productive purpose.

Yet traffic is desperately snarled in many of these cities, and *some* answer to the problem is obviously needed. "The city street has become the Great American Bottleneck; the clog, the snarl, the tangle," says *Architectural Forum.* "It is also the point where the issues of transportation planning are fast becoming the issues of the city's survival."

For many years the solution to congested urban streets was thought to be bigger, better, and more plentiful city streets. Now that "solution" is being challenged. Just as new highways attract new traffic, so new city roads often create new congestion. And there is the additional question of how many roads can be woven through an urban area before the roads take over and the urban quality of the place is shattered. As critic Wolf von Eckardt puts it: "Local highway officials simply refuse to believe that a freeway running through a densely settled neighborhood must be designed differently from a superhighway running through open country."

Then there are economic disadvantages to heavy reliance on freeways. They gobble up land, and generally lower the value of adjoining land, particularly if that land is residential. Each mile of new freeway removes between 40 and 50 acres of taxable property from local tax rolls.

It is of some comfort, however, to those who worry about such things, that the problems aren't all new, or even totally related to the automobile. Some two thousand years ago Julius Caesar banned wheeled vehicles from Rome. And Leonardo da Vinci, designing his ideal city five hundred years ago, talked of the need for split-level streets—high roads for the "convenience of the gentlefolk," low roads for the service and convenience of the common people.

Still, the great debate over freeways and the automobiles continues. In the meantime, all the antiauto arguments fail to dampen the spirits of the automobile makers, or to have any effect whatsoever on the long-standing love affair of the American motorist with his car.

TOLLS COULD EASE THE JAM [2]

What can be done to solve urban transportation problems now?

A transportation expert . . . says solutions, which don't require laying more concrete or extending rail lines, are readily at hand.

[He] feels the answer is to manage the transportation system during the four hours daily that it is strained by commuters squeezing into or out of the city.

According to . . . William E. Griswold of Systems Analysis and Research Corporation: "So much is known about what should be done that continued planning of future solutions cheats the public because it doesn't solve today's problems."

The way he would unsnarl the cities' traffic tie-ups is contained in a report called "The Urban Transportation Dilemma: An Operational Solution." In prepublication excerpts below, he tells how he would reduce the number of vehicles at peak hours:

"The fairest means of accomplishing this would be to establish a system of tolls to divert the least productive vehicles, those carrying only a driver, and encourage more productive vehicles, those carrying several passengers.

"One way of doing this would be to adopt a sliding scale of rush-hour tolls, reducing the toll per vehicle as the number of passengers increases. For example, the toll for cars carrying a driver alone could be set at 50 cents, cars carrying two people would pay 25 cents per car, and cars with three or more passengers would pass free (as would buses and taxis).

"Tolls would be in effect only during the morning rush period, and only in the peak direction of travel."

He says that toll booths could be established at points of entry into the city. In many cities such as Boston, he says, rivers and harbors have reduced the number of entry points

[2] From "Tolls Urged to Ease Traffic Jams," by Richard W. McManus, staff writer. *Christian Science Monitor.* p 18. S. 25, '69. Reprinted by permission from *The Christian Science Monitor* © 1969 The Christian Science Publishing Society. All rights reserved.

to a manageable number and toll stations already exist on some bridges and tunnels.

"The proposed system of variable rush-hour tolls," he says, "would in effect give priority to those vehicles carrying two or more passengers. Commuters driving alone, who are now the majority, would then have four choices:

Continue to drive alone and pay the toll

Drive to a park-and-ride lot outside the toll zone and use public transportation to get downtown

Leave the car at home and travel all the way by public transportation

Find a rider or riders and thereby reduce the toll liability

"While some motorists will respond to peak-hour tolls by forming car pools, parking outside the toll zone, or commuting outside of peak hours, the first and most apparent result of imposing a schedule of tolls ... would be to increase greatly the demand for public transportation (much as when following a snow storm large numbers of motorists choose to leave their cars at home)."

But, since public transportation has no room for these extra passengers during peak hours, he says, a crowded trip becomes jam packed.

Thus, he continues, "it is not surprising that they (motorists) view buses and subways as inacceptable modes of transportation to be endured when necessary, but avoided when possible. Any solution to the problem of traffic congestion therefore must be preceded by a restructuring of public-transportation services to make it possible to accommodate new riders at an acceptable level of comfort."

Mr. Griswold feels the toll policy will produce a need for more transit vehicles. Under present circumstances, management cannot justify the expense, he says.

"However," he explains, "since more effective utilization of the transit system is the key to solving the problem of urban highway congestion, the most productive use for the revenues obtained from peak-hour highway tolls is to apply them to the transit system, thus for the first time giving management the funds necessary to make the improvements which everyone knows are needed, but for which no funding has been available."

Once the toll policy has been put into effect, he says, balance between modes can be easily maintained.

"Should highway demand fall below capacity, rush-hour tolls would simply be adjusted downward until a new equilibrium is achieved. Should transit demand increase more than expected, peak-hour fares, or schedules, or both, can be adjusted until all passengers are accommodated," he concludes.

FIGHTING THE FREEWAY [3]

News of the bulldozer's approach so disturbed a group of Cleveland conservationists that they staged an original protest musical at the neighborhood high school. "We'll barricade the streets like committees of the French," sang a chorus of housewives. "We'll never let the county begin its little trench." A platoon of Harvard students chained themselves to a stand of sycamores in the proposed path of a Cambridge freeway to dramatize their demand for an alternate route. In Washington, resistance leaders didn't bother to be cute; representatives of a Negro area slated for a freeway inundated the Department of Transportation with handbills that said, "No more white highways through black bedrooms."

These are not isolated engagements—but salvos in a war that may well determine the shape of urban America. In no fewer than twenty-five major cities, profreeway and antifreeway forces are locked in bitter power struggles that have escalating implications.

On one side stands what has been labeled "The Freeway Establishment"—state highway commissions, auto clubs, building-and-trades unions, the trucking, petroleum, concrete

---

[3] Article in *Newsweek*. 71:64-5. Mr. 25, '68. Copyright Newsweek, Inc., 1968. Reprinted by permission.

and lumber industries. Lined up in opposition is an alliance of conservationists, landmark preservationists, civil rightists, architects and low-income homeowners to whom the effect of a freeway, in the words of urban critic Lewis Mumford, is like "the passage of a tornado or blast of an atomic bomb."

Standstill—At present, the citizen lobbyists have forced something of a stalemate. In about half the twenty-five cities involved, the 41,000-mile Federal interstate-highway program —which was launched in 1956 and is now 60 per cent completed—has been brought to a standstill. The need for more superhighways is not questioned. A motorist traveling north from Los Angeles on U.S. 101, for example, must detour onto a congested avenue with 36 traffic lights blocking his route up the coast. And with 8 million more cars appearing each year, such "lightmares" are sure to multiply.

What the antifreewayites argue is that highway planning is much too serious to be left to highway engineers and special interests. A single mile of urban expressway, they point out, costs an average of $30 million and chews up 36 to 40 acres of land. Then there is the incalculable cost in ravaged parks and landmarks, in the disruption of thousands of lives to accommodate the automobile.

To be fair, narrow self-interest can also underlie the antifreeway stand. Interstate 696, a twenty-seven-mile expressway designed to skirt the suburban fringe of Detroit, has been effectively roadblocked by the tiniest community along its proposed route, a middle-income oasis named Pleasant Ridge (population: 4,000). While a dozen other towns have granted right of way, Pleasant Ridge has resisted on the ground that surrendering any part of its acreage would threaten its existence as a separate community. "Pleasant Ridge has a history of opposition," claims a state highway official. "They ought to raze it, pave it and turn it into a parking lot."

The freeway furor has generated meaningful new thinking among those who hold the Federal purse strings. In a move that has incensed the highway lobby, Department of

Transportation (DOT) Secretary Alan Boyd . . . [in 1968] threatened to enforce a new law that would withhold Federal funds from projects that fail to allow for sociological, economic and esthetic considerations. That triggered a blast from a spokesman for the Firestone Tire and Rubber Company, who charged that the DOT was "dedicated to the damnation of anything automotive."

More likely, Transportation's stand is inspired by old-fashioned good politics. "The people are not as foolish as we used to think," says one highway planner. "They won't let you shove a plan down their throats any more." Indeed, that point has been so overwhelmingly demonstrated that some planners are despairing of getting any freeways built at all. A tale of five cities:

San Francisco: Ironically, the citizens with the heaviest concentration of cars in the world—7,000 per square mile—fired the first shot in 1959 when they fought the Embarcadero Freeway, an elevated eyesore that would sever most of the city from its view of the bay. Today the Embarcadero stops in midair, mute testimony to the power of protest. Seven years later two more freeways came up for approval, one of which would slash through a distinguished old neighborhood. The proposals stirred San Franciscans anew and at a tumultuous hearing that was packed with oppositionists, the board of supervisors voted 6 to 5 to reject both routes, thus also rejecting $250 million in Federal road-building funds.

Cambridge, Massachusetts: In one of the most heated disputes, five hundred faculty members at Harvard and MIT have petitioned the DOT to reconsider a proposed link of Boston's Inner Belt that would cut a wide swath across Cambridge, displacing some 4,600 persons. The route would primarily benefit middle-income commuters at the expense of low-income residents. In the view of Brandeis sociologist Gordon Fellman, that's not progress. "Why shouldn't the maintenance of stable neighborhoods," he asks, "be of higher value than the whims of the driver?" DOT officials say they are considering alternate routes.

Chicago: Here the issue isn't whether to build or not to build—but whether to build on stilts. And for the first time in the city's history, a proposed highway project—in this case, the towering crosstown "Stiltway"—has been kept on the drawing boards by massive citizen resistance. One neighborhood group marched on City Hall with a silk-lined coffin, chanting, "Don't bury the neighborhood, bury the Stiltway." The Stiltway is quite buried, at least until a newly formed design team agrees on a compromise plan.

New Orleans: "Just when we had them licked," says a stunned highway engineer, "the preservationists have come out smelling like a rose." The engineer had reason for despair. For more than two years, a battle has raged over a proposed elevated expressway that would girdle the historic French Quarter, cutting off Jackson Square from the Mississippi. Calling the plan an "act of barbarism," preservationists have pushed for an alternate ground-level structure that would save the view. Last week [former] Federal Highway Administrator Lowell Bridwell overruled earlier decisions and endorsed the ground-level plan.

Washington: In the climax of a six-year tussle, a Negro group improbably called "Niggers Incorporated," has promised to lie down in front of the bulldozers if planners blast a freeway through a predominantly black neighborhood. DOT Secretary Boyd has adamantly championed their cause, wryly noting that several alternative corridors were rejected after opposition from more influential white residents. "We're going to have to find a better way to build freeways," he says, "than by disrupting those without political clout." The highway industry has zeroed in on the Secretary with its biggest congressional guns. The impasse, they contend, has tied up $800 million in freeway projects. Meanwhile, Boyd has tossed the ball to Walter Washington, the Negro mayor of the District of Columbia. Whatever Washington decides, he is sure to antagonize someone.

Urban Design Concept—To be sure, the resistance has had its setbacks, too. Despite howls, Milwaukee is going ahead with a freeway that will dissect a magnificent park on Lake Michigan. And in Nashville, the courts have approved a controversial highway that would wipe out 80 per cent of a Negro-owned business district. But thanks to sympathizers like Boyd, the Federal Government is beginning to consider new approaches.

The most promising of these bears the unwieldy name of "urban design concept team." Conceived by Baltimore architect Archibald Rogers, it brings together a team of specialists—engineers, architects, sociologists, acoustical and pollution experts—to anticipate the impact of a proposed route on every facet of community life. Thus the team might decide to tunnel a freeway beneath a park, or construct housing projects along its right of way or link it with a mass-transit system at the city limits (the "park and ride" approach).

Air Rights—Although highway engineers are edgy about sharing their hegemony with what one calls "petunia planters, bird watchers and do-gooders," design teams are already forming in Boston, Chicago and Seattle. New York is employing one to develop its "linear city," perhaps the boldest highway project extant. Using the air rights over a proposed stretch of expressway in Brooklyn, the city is planning to string out apartments, schools and shopping plazas over the actual road. Critics have suggested that linear city be renamed "carbon monoxide city." But as city planner Edward Robin sees it, the concept could weld together a totally new community instead of tearing an old one apart. [The plan has since been scrapped.—Ed.]

Budgetary limitations and bureaucratic intransigence remain the major roadblocks to such innovations. Meanwhile, the production of new cars outstrips the birth rate and the flow of concrete lava threatens to engulf the landscape. A score of communities have decided to hold out for humane highway planning whatever the cost. For the rest, getting from here to there still appears to be the prime concern—but what if nothing is there?

TOO MUCH FOR HIGHWAYS [4]

Congress and the American people are nearing a fundamental decision on transportation policy revolving about the Highway Trust Fund, which is scheduled to go out of existence on September 30, 1972. The Nixon Administration has asked Congress to extend it for another four years, and House and Senate committees have begun hearings.

Established in 1956 to finance the Interstate Highway System, the fund is fed by the Federal tax of 4 cents a gallon on gasoline and by lesser excise taxes. Since this money can only be used to build new highways and since the Federal Government pays 90 per cent of the construction, the mere existence of the fund is a self-perpetuating engine which generates tremendous pressure on the states to go ahead with ever more ambitious road projects. The fund's annual revenue now approximates $5 billion and over the next several years will inexorably rise to $6.5 billion. Is it really necessary to spend this vast sum each year on new highways?

By contrast, only $156 million was spent in the last year in Federal aid for subways, buslines and other forms of urban mass transit. In the past dozen years, $50 billion has been spent to build highways, fifty times as much as the Federal Government has devoted to mass transit. It is now expected that the Interstate Highway System will cost almost twice the original estimate—$75 billion instead of $41 billion.

It is not public policy for Congress to freeze such large tax revenues in any fund devoted to a single narrow purpose. But Congress has become wedded to the trust fund concept, and private interest group pressures make its abolition highly unlikely. This year a fund to finance airports was created.

As a practical matter, the issue before Congress is whether the highway and airport funds can be broadened into a single Transportation Trust Fund. Urban mass transit, railroad passenger service and other transport needs could then

---

[4] Editorial. New York *Times*. p 38. Jl. 29, '70. © 1970 by The New York Times Company. Reprinted by permission.

be considered and reconciled in accordance with a rational plan. The bankruptcy of the Penn Central, the inadequate service on the Long Island Rail Road and other commuter railroads, the headlong decline in railroad passenger service and its actual disappearance in many states, the ever-intensifying traffic jams in every city, and the shortage and undependability of bus service in both cities and suburban towns are the exhausting evidence of the lack of a coherent policy.

The nation's governors and mayors are urging Congress to introduce flexibility into the operations of the highway fund. They want each state to have the option to use part of its Federal highway funds for mass transit. Representative Edward I. Koch of Manhattan and other members of Congress are pushing bills to allocate the 7 per cent auto excise tax, which now goes into the Treasury's general revenues, to a new Urban Mass Transportation Trust Fund as a transitional step toward a merger of all the transportation funds. Senator Jennings Randolph of West Virginia has introduced a modest measure to permit the diversion of Federal highway funds for operation—but not construction—of mass transit in urban areas.

Secretary of Transportation John A. Volpe is well aware of these rising pressures. But he has been notably timid in offering any leadership for reform. In presenting the Administration recommendations for extension of the Highway Trust Fund, he recognized the desirability of balancing mass transit against the imperious demand of the truck and the private automobile but he ventured nothing more than a pious acknowledgment. He suggested no change except to make safety research and the pathetically starved program for removal of billboards eligible for comparatively small sums from the Highway Trust Fund.

Naturally this feeble proposal evoked ritualistic outcries from those well-known enemies of common sense, Representatives John C. Kluczynski, the Chicago Democrat who is chairman of the roads subcommittee, and William C. Cramer, the Florida Republican who is the ranking minority member. Messrs. Kluczynski and Cramer have been vocal and attentive servitors of the highway lobby for many years.

If Secretary Volpe defaults to the highway lobby, the nonpolicy of the last fifteen years will continue to prevail with increasingly disastrous consequences. The time of decision is rapidly approaching. Whenever it comes, the battle for a rational, balanced transportation policy, is sure to be hard and bruising. The longer Secretary Volpe is timid and evasive the less likely is a victory for the public good.

ANOTHER $320 BILLION FOR ROADS? [5]

Big decisions—and a hot battle—involving the nation's multibillion-dollar highway program are shaping up in Washington.

State highway commissioners are now asking that outlays on roads be nearly doubled in the years ahead.

They want the state and the Federal Government to boost spending on highways from about $11 billion a year now to more than 21 billion a year in the fifteen years between now and 1985. Grand total for the period: 320 billion, if these state officials get all they want.

With that money, the states say they would build 53,000 miles of new freeways through the country, improve tens of thousands of miles of roads of less-than-freeway dimensions, correct 180,000 unprotected railroad crossings, replace 89,000 bridges that are deemed to be unsafe or inadequate, and develop a vast new system of expressways in the metropolitan areas.

About 29 billions of the total would go to complete the 42,500-mile Interstate Highway System that was begun in 1956. At that time, this program was billed as the greatest public-works project in history. Its cost was forecast at $27 billion, and it was to be finished in 1971. As things stand

[5] Reprinted from article "320 Billion Dollars More for Future Highways?" *U.S. News & World Report.* 68:34-5. Mr. 2, '70.

now, the interstate network will have taken about 70 billion by the time it is completed—and that won't be until around 1977, six years late.

Congress faces decisions long before that, however. The present highway law expires within a year, and pressure is growing not only to extend it, but to prepare an even bigger program to follow. Engineers contend at least five years will be needed to make detailed plans, acquire land and begin placing contracts.

As a starter, the American Association of State Highway Officials says Congress should vote the states three quarters of a billion dollars just for planning future roads, with the first 250 million to become available the year after next.

New Roadblocks?

The states' dreams of a vast new building boom run headlong into mounting opposition, both private and official.

Some Federal experts say the United States already spends too much money on highways, and that some of these funds should be diverted to improve public transportation, especially rapid transit.

A Senate subcommittee headed by Senator William Proxmire (Democrat, Wisconsin) wants Congress to abolish the present Highway Trust Fund, on the theory that this move would lead to tighter control over the Federal outlays for road building. And the Secretary of Transportation, John A. Volpe, suggests there should be a "transportation fund" that would help pay for mass transit and airports, as well as highways.

In the cities . . . there is stiff resistance to building more freeways through settled neighborhoods, where houses have to be torn down and where residents worry about noise, fumes and the traffic that tends to spill into adjoining areas.

On February 16 [1970], Secretary Volpe announced tough regulations requiring that housing be provided for families displaced by transportation projects, and he indicated that the Highway Trust Fund might be tapped to pay for acquiring the substitute homes. Mr. Volpe also ruled that, starting in July, states must share this expense.

Mounting Concern

Outside the cities, conservationists criticize the impact of new highways on woodlands, wildlife and drainage.

Increasingly, there is concern that the process of building superhighways may have no end. More roads seem to generate more traffic, which in turn requires more roads. This worry is not relieved by the states' estimate that $320 billion will be required for highway construction in the next fifteen years.

The $11 billion a year the states, cities and Federal Government are spending at present for roads and streets is not much more than half the rate the states say will be necessary to take care of the "needs" they now anticipate. Where would the additional money come from?

Federal taxes on motor fuel, motor oil, tires, tubes, tread rubber, trucks, buses, trailers and accessories funnel nearly $5 billion a year into the Federal Highway Trust Fund. State and local levies dedicated to road programs bring in about another 5 billion.

Revenues, of course, will increase with the number of vehicles in use and the amount of driving. The Federal taxes, for instance, are expected to rise to 7.3 billions in 1985.

By then, the experts predict, the United States will have 143.5 million motor vehicles on the roads, 38.5 million more than today. The amount of travel is forecast at 1.5 trillion miles per year, up from about a trillion now.

An additional source of revenue could be new or increased taxes. The President has asked Congress to boost the levies on diesel fuel and on heavy trucks to the tune of 259 millions a year.

Even so, Federal officials say they do not see where money will be available for half the work the states want to do.

Meanwhile, the cost of construction keeps on climbing. The average mile of road now costs about a third more than it did in 1959. The rise, just since 1968, has been about 7 per cent.

Change of Emphasis

Highway planners, when they started the interstate program in 1956, had a relatively simple mission: to provide a network of freeways connecting all major population centers.

National defense was advanced as one reason for the project, and the Federal Government agreed to pay 90 per cent of the expense.

The program now being urged by the states is more complex. It would rely, as the present building does, on the Highway Trust Fund, but the Federal share is expected to be about 70 per cent, leaving 30 per cent to be paid by states and localities.

State engineers give top priority to 53,000 miles of roads that are not part of the interstate system. These arteries, officials say, often carry more traffic than the freeways that have had the lion's share of Federal support. In general, they would be brought up to freeway standards.

Cities' Needs

There is broad agreement, too, among the engineers that cities will need a vast amount of help. New interstate roads are dumping traffic into congested sections faster than they can handle it. Only 13 per cent of streets and expressways in urban areas are now eligible for Federal aid. Yet these areas have 70 per cent of the nation's population and are expected to account for 80 per cent by 1980.

Figures supplied by the states indicate the metropolitan centers will need $123 billion in the next two decades to solve their transportation problems—90 billion for streets and expressways and 33 billion for mass-transit systems.

That division of funds between the two forms of transport is causing much controversy. The President's budget contains this warning:

"Expenditures on one mode of transportation often affect other modes as well. For example, a new urban highway may encourage users of mass transit to commute by driving, thus placing the suppliers of mass transit in financial straits and causing traffic congestion."

Arguments in some cities are so intense that officials say about 150 miles of interstate freeways, already planned for the cities, may never be built.

Better Busways?

In their future designs, the highway engineers expect to place greater stress on buses, which move more people over a given amount of road space. Few cities, these officials say, are large enough to support rail systems, but most can benefit from better bus service.

Thus, expressways in urban areas are more likely to include lanes for the exclusive use of buses in rush hours. A demonstration of this kind of service is now being developed for the heavily used Shirley Highway, leading into Washington, D. C., from the south.

Large suburban parking areas are to be built at bus terminals, in the hope that more people will use the public transit for the major part of their travel to and from work. Similar projects are planned for other cities.

More beltways, farther out from the most congested urban areas, also are in the highway engineers' plans.

Construction of additional bridges will cost nearly $19 billion, the states say. That includes replacing nearly 89,000 existing bridges and building nine hundred completely new crossings.

The replacements grow out of studies that were made after the collapse of the Silver Bridge across the Ohio River took forty-six lives in 1967.

All this needs to be done, the state engineers say, in the interest of safety and better movement of people and products. The huge road-building boom they urge would also provide tens of thousands of jobs and absorb vast amounts of cement, steel and construction equipment.

Thus, the stakes are high as the battle over the future highway program begins.

III. COMMUTING IN METROPOLIS

EDITOR'S INTRODUCTION

The transit task in metropolitan areas is twofold: moving those who live on the fringes into the inner city, and circulating those in the core city to and from their work, homes, and other activities. Both parts of the job offer vast room for improvement before the United States will have first-class mass transit.

Commuter railroad lines and commuter bus lines face chronic deficits. Many are subsidized by city and state governments. Inner-city transit lines are generally decayed, and often continue to serve the wrong areas long after city development has moved to different sections. Many lines require heavy subsidies to continue running. Some are owned outright by the cities.

There are exceptions to the list of poor facilities: San Francisco is building a well-coordinated system (BART—Bay Area Rapid Transit) that reaches out into adjoining counties. Philadelphia and Chicago have money-making commuter rail lines.

The first article in this section, from *Business Week,* concentrates on the plight of commuter railroads. The focus is on the Penn Central Railroad, which has now gone into bankruptcy. The next article traces the development and decline of commuter railroads serving a suburban area of New Jersey. From Philadelphia, the next article offers a happier tale: a very successful new suburban rail line.

Most writers on mass transit pay scant attention to buses —yet the unglamorous fact is that about 75 per cent of all U.S. mass transit consists of buses. An article from the Bergen County (New Jersey) *Record* details the difficulties bus lines actively competing for passengers face in one suburban area.

James Clayton's article delves into the parallel experiences of two big cities now constructing advanced new transit systems: San Francisco and Washington. And, from *Fortune,* the final article in the section describes an exemplary new subway that not only works but is beautiful to behold. Unfortunately, this paragon is not in the United States but in Mexico City.

THE STORY BEHIND THE COMMUTER CRISIS [1]

It is hard for a commuter to know whom to blame when his trains consistently run late, break down, or otherwise fall dismally short of the ideal. A railroad is a complex operation which can come unscrewed in any number of ways; when even the conductor does not know (or will not tell) the reason for the latest delay, it may seem to be a matter of impersonal fate—another failure in some fundamentally unworkable "system." But a great many commuters of late have found a personal target for their frustrations in the person of Stuart Thomas Saunders, the imperious sixty-year-old chairman of Penn Central Company.

Invective and abuse have been heaped on Saunders because of the deteriorating service that the Penn Central provides for its 300,000 commuters in New York and Philadelphia. Beyond that, the lawyer-turned-railroad-man displays a bluntly unsympathetic attitude, which helps to make him a lightning rod for commuter criticism. Asked why the Penn Central was not investing more money on commuter operations, Saunders once told a visitor: "You wouldn't do it. I won't do it. I'd be crazy to do a thing like that. The stockholders would never get a penny back." [Soon after this article appeared, Saunders was replaced as Penn Central chairman; the railroad went into bankruptcy proceedings.—Ed.]

The cruel truth is that Saunders' viewpoint (if not his public relations sense) is hard to dispute. Commuter opera-

[1] From article in *Business Week.* p 60-71. Mr. 14, '70. Reprinted from the March 14, 1970, issue of *Business Week* by special permission. Copyrighted © 1970 by McGraw-Hill, Inc.

tions can no longer be carried out economically by a privately owned railroad—and what is happening on the Penn Central is a portent of what is to come on every commuter road in the United States. The Penn Central commuter service has become the most horrible—and visible—example of a business that is in fatal trouble.

Inflation, tight money, and steadily aging equipment have brought the commuter problem to a crisis. Some kind of milestone was set last January 9, when the Penn Central hit a new low in performance. On its Philadelphia lines, the road canceled 117 trains, and of the 296 trains that did run 290 were late.

And more is involved in the crisis than the complaints of unhappy riders. Most major cities are strangling in auto traffic, and some form of mass transportation is desperately needed. Rail service, which does not pollute the air, may become essential for many U.S. cities besides the five (New York, Philadelphia, Boston, Chicago, and San Francisco) where railroads now supply commuter service.

But a fundamental question has arisen over the position of the privately owned railroad: How does it balance its duty to the public against its responsibility to make profits for stockholders?

There is not much that can be done under existing law to force a railroad to provide the sort of service commuters feel they are entitled to. Commuter service is "basically unprofitable," says Paul W. Cherington, professor of transportation at Harvard University and formerly assistant secretary for policy and international affairs of the Transportation Department. "I don't see why any private corporation should be required to maintain a basically losing operation."

The High Cost of Railroading

The capital costs of the rail plant used in commuter service are difficult, if not impossible, to amortize because the plant is fully utilized only about twenty hours a week—during morning and evening rush hours, Monday through Friday.

For the rest of the week, acres of cars and miles of track lie idle.

The service is labor intensive, requiring thousands of conductors, brakemen, motormen, ticket punchers, ticket sellers, and repairmen. With the train crews, the problem is exacerbated by a service that requires them to perform their duties at either end of their customers' eight-hour days. Well-established working agreements protected by powerful unions see to it that crews are well paid for these split shifts and also make any changes in the work rules all but impossible.

Finally, commuter pricing goes counter to economic principles in that rush-hour service, which is the most expensive to provide, is sold at a discount rather than a premium. In fact, the peaks and valleys of commuter traffic are so sharp that while additional riders at off-peak hours go far to reduce losses, extra riders in the rush hour actually add to the deficit (assuming there are enough to require putting on extra equipment).

Only a few years ago, service on at least some of the present Penn Central lines was both reliable and reasonably comfortable. And some parts of the country—notably around Chicago and on the San Francisco peninsula—still have good commuting. Where good service is provided, the providers expect to get something in return. "It can be a matter of deliberate strategy to improve the commuter business," says Cherington, "if you can trade off the money it takes for something you really need."

The Southern Pacific south of San Francisco and most of the railroads around Chicago have invested heavily in commuter operations, and they see good suburban service as returning valuable benefits other than financial. They provide the service to please important segments of their public—their officers and directors, bankers, investors, shippers, local politicians—or simply because they want to be regarded as a good corporate neighbor.

The president of one Chicago-based railroad says that one rather important reason his railroad has spent so much money and effort on the suburban service is that, "Periodically Dick Daley [Chicago Mayor Richard J. Daley] comes around to my office and tells me we've got to. And when Dick Daley tells us to do something, we generally find it worthwhile to do it."

Aside from the fact that there is only one Mayor Daley, why didn't the Penn Central invest heavily in commuter equipment, as the Western railroads did? "They didn't have the money," says Cherington.

Says William B. Johnson, a former Pennsylvania Railroad lawyer, now chairman of Illinois Central Industries, Inc., and one of the most respected thinkers in the industry:

The Penn Central has got to spend $500 million a year on capital projects if it wants to keep its freight service competitive with other railroads and with modern trucks on interstate highways. Yet it can only scrape up about $290 million a year. It's got its shippers who depend on it. It's got its employees to think about. It's got to spend that money where it will do the most good.

John A. Bailey, director of Northwestern University's Transportation Center and a former general manager of the Southeastern Pennsylvania Transportation Authority (SEPTA), agrees that rail commuter service is unprofitable under existing ground rules. He says it could be made profitable by charging much higher fares and forcing drivers to pay the full cost of driving into the center city. But he also thinks that railroads in the commuter business, and specifically the Penn Central, have "an implied obligation to run something." They operate as a common carrier under a public certificate of convenience and necessity, he points out, and the public has a right to expect service in return for this certificate. "Realistically though," he adds, "there isn't any way to force them to operate a quality service."

Ever since a 1958 amendment to the Interstate Commerce Act spelled out the relationship between Federal and state regulatory agencies concerned with abandonment of commuter operations, the act has been the overriding authority in this area. And there is nothing in it that says that a commuter railroad must provide frequent, reliable service in new equipment. Last fall, in fact, in a case involving long-haul passenger service, the Interstate Commerce Commission specifically rejected the idea that it had the authority to regulate the quality of service, although it did ask Congress to give it such authority.

In many cases, state and local regulation of commuter service is more stringent than Federal regulation. But there are some questions as to whether the state regulations can be enforced if they can be shown to be damaging to a corporation engaged in interstate commerce, as a railroad that operates freight service is.

Both the Public Service Commission of New York and the Public Utility Commission of Pennsylvania have taken action to investigate the "character and standard of service" provided on Penn Central commuter lines. New York's PSC has an order dating back to last summer requiring the Penn Central to acquire eighty new cars and to meet minimum standards of cleanliness and on-time performance. The railroad, which is negotiating with the state's Metropolitan Transportation Authority to operate its Hudson and Harlem division commuter lines under contract to the MTA, has refused the PSC order on the grounds that they will be acquired under the MTA contract. . . .

But in any case, it is by no means a legal certainty that a state commission has the power to force a railroad to buy new equipment or even to improve the quality of service. "They're trying to use the courts in Philadelphia to force the Penn Central to provide a certain quality of service," Bailey says. "I don't think they can win."

Bailey, who as general manager of Pennsylvania's SEPTA negotiated subsidy payments for both railroads, compares Penn Central's attitude unfavorably with that of Philadelphia's other commuter railroad, the Reading. "The Reading made a sincere attempt to find out what the customers want and tailor the service accordingly," he says. "Any zest for that has been lost on the Penn Central."

It is not only a matter of attitude, it is also a matter of money. The Penn Central, which operates a third of the nation's commuter service (and the same proportion of the even more unprofitable long-haul passenger service), clearly is vulnerable to the money crunch. Its railroad operations overall, including freight and long-haul passenger as well as commuter lines, are only marginally profitable.

The combined losses on commuter and intercity passenger service can occasionally add up to more than the profit on freight operations. So, many years ago the Penn Central's predecessors began to look for ways to get rid of the losses in passenger operations in order to preserve freight service on a competitive basis.

The problem was more urgent with Penn Central and other Eastern roads than with some of the Western lines because the Eastern roads have relatively less opportunity to do what railroads do best and most profitably—haul large numbers of freight cars for very long distances without tieing them up in expensive terminal operations.

Ending Major Losses

A long-haul railroad like the Southern Pacific—which has a net income of around $100 million a year, year-in and year-out—can find ways to absorb the cost of a commuter operation that racks up annual deficits of about $1 million. And it may count the money well spent for good will. But even the immensely profitable Southern Pacific, when it became clear that long-haul passenger operations would suck tens of millions of dollars annually out of its treasury, moved quickly to discontinue long-haul service.

The largest commuting deficits are racked up by railroads that have not modernized equipment to improve efficiency. Where a service has been modernized, or where a new line has been built from scratch, commuter services can be operated at close to the break-even point, or even at a small operating profit. But the profit of even the most efficient commuter operation—given a fare-structure that has to compete with the low out-of-pocket cost to a driver of an auto trip—is far less than can be earned on an investment in almost any phase of rail freight operations. Commuter service can never provide sufficient return on investment to generate its own source of new capital—and with competition for freight business growing more intense every year, a loss leader such as an efficient commuter operation becomes harder and harder to support.

This is why Penn Central's Saunders has chosen to concentrate nearly all the road's capital investment in freight. The inevitable result has been a dwindling supply of passenger cars as more and more pass the point where they can be repaired or spend an increasing amount of time in the shop. On the Penn Central's Westchester lines, for instance, current timetables call for more trains and more frequent service now than ten years ago, though only about 400 cars are available compared with about 900 in 1960.

But as deteriorating equipment, compounded by cold weather, made a mockery of Penn Central commuter schedules this winter, one danger of the freight-concentration policy quickly became evident. The railroad began to draw blasts of criticism from powerful and articulate people, including partners of influential law firms, editors, television executives, advertising agency officials, bankers, brokers, and others among the nation's movers and shakers.

In defending themselves, Penn Central officials argue that the money to rehabilitate commuter service should come from the communities it serves rather than from the railroad. They point out that per capita wealth and income in Westport, Darien, and Greenwich, in Scarsdale, Chappaqua, and Ossining, in Princeton and Bryn Mawr, are far above the average of U.S. communities. Yet, say railroad officers, these communities have never been willing to support the full costs of good commuter service, which include periodic buying of new commuter equipment. Even fare increases designed only to keep up with inflation have been bitterly opposed.

In the end it becomes a question of responsibility. Who has the right to do what, when, where, and to whom? It is not an easy question to answer.

Penn Central's critics feel that the company's overwhelming devotion to stockholder interest borders on an unreasonable preoccupation with profit to the exclusion of other corporate responsibilities.

The argument is that commuter service is a legitimate public interest which is the joint responsibility of the lines and concerned government bodies. Where there is a conflict between public interest and stockholder interest, the corporate charter has to be balanced against the corporate duty to act responsibly in the business for which it is chartered. As one critic puts it, "I'm not quibbling over their day-to-day service this winter. I'm upset by what I consider a lack of vision and an unwillingness to accept any social responsibility for contributing to the environment in which they expect to prosper."

Penn Central's vice president for passenger services, Howard C. Kohout, admits that the railroad has made a lot of riders very unhappy. "I'm not saying the public doesn't have reason to complain," he says. "They do. But the public has taken an apathetic view. In all the major cities, they've found the money to build highways and sports arenas and all kinds of things on which there is no return, but they've been very backward in finding ways to help move people."

Kohout and other Penn Central people insist that the railroad had given the public full warning that suburban service was on a collision course with disaster. "A lot of people felt we were whistling by the cemetery," Kohout says. "We weren't. A lot of people think that just because the 5:03 ran yesterday, it's going to run every day without anybody doing anything to keep it running."

A. Sheffer Lang of the Massachusetts Institute of Technology, formerly the Federal Railroad Administrator, agrees that a railroad's primary responsibility is to its stockholders. But if it comes to a showdown between the interests of the stockholders and the general public, he points out, legislators will see to it that the public ultimately comes out on top. Lang suggests it is probably impossible to represent the real interest of the stockholder without taking into account the public interest. And he adds, "Where I part company with Saunders and others like him is, what kind of balance between the conflicting interests it is proper to strike."

Says John Kohl, New Jersey's new transportation commissioner and formerly administrator of the Federal mass transit aid program: "Clearly, railroads have a responsibility, direct or implied. They were given power and privileges in return for agreeing to provide public service." But, Kohl adds, "The public can't expect them to continue to perform indefinitely at a loss." New Jersey has recognized this concept for years. Since 1961, the state has paid $78.4 million to Jersey railroads as a direct subsidy for providing commuter service.

This subsidy, in fact, has been an important reason why commuting on the Erie-Lackawanna railway is consistently more reliable than on the Penn Central during sieges of bad weather. When snow starts to fall, Erie-Lackawanna officials can, and frequently do, call out crews to man light engines in the middle of the night. These locomotives run up and down the line keeping tracks clear and switches open for the morning rush. The cost of this is part of the total operating loss and is passed along to New Jersey taxpayers.

The Penn Central, on the other hand, would rather turn over commuter operations to an authority than rely on subsidies to make up deficits. The railroad feels that subsidies are inadequate and believes that interim measures will only put off the day when state agencies take over the commuter service. But service got so bad from Westchester County into New York this winter that it became a political liability to New York's Governor Nelson A. Rockefeller, who . . . [was] running for reelection. So Rockefeller, Saunders, Penn Central President Paul A. Gorman, and the line's senior vice president for law, Robert W. Minor, went into a hurry-up meeting.

The meeting was at least partly responsible for an emergency $30.7 million transit aid loan, passed by the state legislature at Rockefeller's request. Of this, $7.3 million is earmarked for stopgap measures to recondition Penn Central cars, locomotives, and stations. But major relief is still dependent on passing responsibility for the service on to the MTA. And, given present lead time on car orders, this means that relief is at least two years away—even if the negotiations could be concluded immediately, which is quite unlikely.

The New Yorker who sees his Chicago counterpart sitting in clean, well-lighted equipment that operates on reliable schedules when he, himself, is standing in—or frequently in the vestibule of—a dark and dirty car that is seldom on time, might well ask what makes Chicago a special case.

The biggest—and best publicized—success story of commuting belongs to [chairman] Ben W. Heineman's Chicago & North Western Railway. In the 1950s, the C&NW operated what its own people now concede was a "rotten" service. It had old equipment drawn by steam locomotives, and it made a lot of close-in stops in competition with the Chicago Transit Authority.

Then, in 1957, the road went to the Illinois Commerce Commission with proposals for a major revision of its passenger service. In return for being allowed to drop practically all long-distance trains, for being permitted to close 22 close-in stations out of the total 88 suburban stations on the railroad, for getting the right to increase commuter fares and revise collection procedures, Heineman promised to thoroughly modernize the commuter service. The commission bought the package and the railroad placed the first orders for what eventually amounted to $60 million worth of new diesels and bilevel cars capable of carrying about two thirds again as many passengers as a conventional coach.

To go along with the bilevel cars, North Western management developed "push-pull," a technique that allows diesel-powered commuter trains to be operated in either direction without turning, thus gaining the flexibility and efficiency of electrically powered multiple unit cars without the cost of electrification. All of the C&NW's commuter trains have been bilevel, push-pull since 1961—a major factor in keeping operating expenses under control.

Eliminating most of the long-distance passenger losses, and the huge maintenance costs of the old steam-hauled commuter service, created a very dramatic turnaround in the C&NW's earnings. The stock of what was then a very thinly capitalized railroad took off like a rocket. With soaring per share earnings, Heineman was able to acquire a number of companies from outside the railroad industry. His company quickly became a conglomerate and changed its name to Northwest Industries.

But the turnaround in the railroad that sparked the first boom in the stock is no longer there. In fact, most analysts now consider the road an albatross for Heineman, and he is trying to sell it off to the Chicago, Milwaukee, St. Paul & Pacific Railroad.

Playing With the Numbers

Though the North Western has claimed profits from its commuter operations every year but two since 1959, with an estimated $2 million net in 1969 from suburban service, most other Chicago railroad officials don't believe it. "If you want me to sit here and tell you for the record that Ben Heineman puts some suburban service costs where they don't belong, I'm not going to do it," says one. Then he adds, "But it's true. Ben hasn't charged station costs against the suburban service in ten years." This the C&NW indignantly denies.

An Illinois Central man says, "North Western has always put up this big front that railroads could make money on commuters if they only knew how to operate, but they've never let anybody see their books." Another railroad executive says, "The North Western's claims of $2 million profits are the biggest smile in the railroad industry. We lose $500,000 a year on our commuter operations, and the North Western has the same problems."

As MIT's Lang puts it, "The North Western, for its own good reasons, has been careful to make the operation look as profitable as possible." Lang, who says he sees "no argument moral or otherwise" to fault them for it, describes the C&NW decision to invest in commuter equipment and good service as reasonable "because they knew they had to operate the service and that the general opinion of the railroad would be conditioned by the quality of the service."

C&NW's motives were "reasonably transparent," Lang says. "They needed public approbation for discontinuance of long-distance trains; they bought the public favor." He adds that there can be a significant advantage to a railroad in being able to do well a job that the public considers necessary. "For a public-service industry, this is very important," he says.

Says another Chicago railroad official, "Heineman made a conscious decision to make people think he had rehabilitated his entire railroad by rehabilitating the hell out of the 2 per cent most people see." This man admits to a certain pique when people at cocktail parties or the Chicago Club tell him what a great railroad the C&NW is. "I ask them if it's a profitable railroad," he says, "and they tell me it must be because if Heineman can run commuter service so efficiently and so profitably, the rest of it has to be profitable." Actually, the C&NW overall railroad operations racked up a loss of $18.2 million in 1969.

"It may be the best commuter railroad in the country but it certainly can't be accounted an outstanding financial success," says Lang. And a C&NW man admits that "the return on investment is peanuts. No businessman would buy our service." He adds that the line is constantly running scared. "There are so many things that can upset a commuter service. No matter how good you are today, tomorrow you've got to do it all over again."

And even the C&NW has difficulty finding money for new passenger equipment. Five cars now on order were financed by a loan from Metropolitan Life Insurance Company, using the cars as collateral. Like every other borrower, C&NW has had to pay very high interest rates and is worried about where future money will come from.

The line is concerned also about competition from the city-owned and subsidized Chicago Transit Authority, which is stretching its lines out along new expressways into C&NW territory. A spokesman says "There's only a limited number of passengers; if CTA gets them, they won't ride us. No region can afford the luxury of two lines competing with each other. They should be coordinated."

Given C&NW's admitted concern about subsidized competition and the losses of its railroad operations, it came as no great surprise to railroaders when the C&NW last month proposed that a superagency be created to handle all of the Chicago region's mass transit.

The initial proposal came from Larry S. Provo, C&NW president, who said,

We believe . . . that public subsidies for mass transit will increase substantially. . . . The North Western does not wish to oppose such subsidies. However, it cannot survive as a private enterprise in competition with mass transit fortified by an intensive infusion of Federal, state, and local funds.

C&NW had developed a plan, Provo said, calling for establishing a Chicago Area Transportation Authority which would have "the authority to purchase, lease, operate, and contract for operation of all the transportation facilities involved in mass transit in the metropolitan area of Chicago." This would include bus lines, suburban railroads, the CTA, and possibly highway improvements, Provo said. "To bring this about," he added, "the North Western is ready to sell its suburban lines and equipment to such an authority, and, if so desired, continue to operate it on a contractual basis."

There is pretty general agreement on the desirability of a central authority to coordinate transportation in the Chicago area, but not on how its formation could be accomplished. "The idea is a good one," says George DeMent, chairman of the CTA. "But it would be a Herculean task and would require massive funds." Asked why the North Western ventured the suggestion, DeMent chuckled. "I don't think I should make a judgment on why they did it," he said. "Ask Provo whether he's worried about his finances."

A Burlington spokesman says: "We agree in principle with this wide-area proposal, but we have no plans to surrender our control over either the right-of-way or train operations." The Burlington thinks, he says, that a detailed study could resolve the conflicts and is "not shutting the door at all."

Alan S. Boyd, president of the Illinois Central, observes, "Transportation is a regional problem and should be handled as such. If it appears that public ownership of our commuter service is preferable to private operation, we would cooperate. . . . But we would not approve any piecemeal solution."

The Illinois Central commuter service operated in the red until about three years ago, a spokesman says, when the lower labor costs generated by a newly installed automatic fare-collection system made it possible to show a small out-of-pocket profit. "Now it's down to almost nothing because of salary increases," he says.

The IC is happy when its commuter services break even, but the road has no illusions about the basic nature of the business. "There is no way to run a commuter service in private enterprise," IC Chairman Johnson says flatly. He adds, "If the people don't want railroads as private enterprises, they should nationalize them. The railroads can't live in this never-never land forever."

The IC already participates in a public transit district. Under contract with Chicago South Suburban Mass Transit District, it will obtain this fall 123 new bilevel cars costing

$38 million, $25.2 million of which is Federal funds, with the balance paid by IC as an advance lease payment on the cars. The other major commuter roads in Chicago are headed in the same direction. The Burlington, which started the renaissance in Chicago commuting in 1950 when it bought thirty air-conditioned bilevel cars, is asking the suburban communities it serves to form a transit district eligible for Federal aid. The Milwaukee, which carries its 23,000 daily riders on about a break-even basis, says it too wants to form a transit district. And the financially ailing Rock Island, which says it loses about $700,000 a year on commuter service, sees such action as a necessary future step.

Whether in Chicago, New York, or Philadelphia, there are signs that the public honeymoon with the superhighway as a transit facility is ending. As the expressways become more congested, increasing numbers of people want to return to mass transit. In the smaller metropolitan areas, probably the most efficient form of mass transit is, and will continue to be, by bus—perhaps with freeway express lanes reserved exclusively for bus operations. Ten years from now, there may be a new "dual-mode guideway" technology available that will combine the convenience of private vehicles with the efficiency of guided transit lanes.

But for now, in the four or five areas in which commuting density on individual routes is 15,000 riders an hour or more, rail transit is an admitted public necessity. And as the readiness of the Chicago area roads to participate in transit districts demonstrates, some form of public assistance will be required for any road to survive. With the Nixon Administration's $3.1 billion transit aid program likely to pass in some form or other, major funds are in sight. The question is what form the public authority should take. [The bill was passed by both houses of Congress and signed by President Nixon on October 15, 1970.—Ed.]

Looking to the Future

An agency that will certainly be closely examined as a possible prototype is New York's MTA, set up in 1968 to run the Long Island Rail Road, the New York city-owned subways and buses, some of the areas's bridges and tunnels, and small-plane airports. A true superauthority, the MTA is also—thanks to the passage in 1967 of a $2.5 billion transportation bond referendum—in the happy position of having money already allocated for transportation improvements. But just as it takes years for commuter cars to be manufactured after they have been ordered, it will be years before the MTA can function fully.

The authority got off to a bad start. MTA Chairman William J. Ronan made some strategic errors in working out a labor problem that was strangling car repairs. When no progress was made and service plummeted, Governor Rockefeller was forced to take a hand personally. In a flash of campaign rhetoric—Rockefeller . . . [faced] the loss of normally Republican Long Island in his upcoming bid for re-election because of failing commuter service—the governor promised that the Long Island would be the best railroad in the country within sixty days. Service is much improved since his intervention, but the railroad is still far from being a good one, let alone the best in the country.

Now the authority is on the track. Whether it is the right one remains to be seen. Sometime this spring [1970], MTA Chairman Ronan will sign a formal agreement with the Penn Central for MTA, along with the Connecticut Transportation Authority, to take over the former New Haven commuter service. (The bankrupt NH became part of Penn Central two years ago, and its bad commuter service has been getting worse ever since.)

When the contract is signed, MTA and CTA can begin spending about $56.8 million in Federal and state funds for New Haven rehabilitation, including purchase of 144 new cars. Later, when MTA and Penn Central reach agreement on MTA assistance in operating the Hudson and Harlem divisions, PC will get MTA funds that will make improved service possible on those lines.

The thing that's wrong with commuter service [says Ronan] is that we've had fifty years of neglect. We're working our way out of the awful hole caused by half a century of run-down equipment, inadequate management, and commuter operations that were never designed for transit operations in the first place.

Ronan cites the much publicized difficulties of the Budd-built Metropolitan cars for the Long Island Rail Road as an example of the problems commuter operations face. "America's much-vaunted technology just isn't as good as it ought to be," he says.

Ronan is all-powerful in dictating the policies of his agency . . . and he has been heavily criticized by commuters and in the press as a result of recent fare increases on the LIRR. The MTA chairman says that these were "absolutely necessary." The LIRR, he says, "was starved for thirty years under PSC regulation and things went right down the drain. What the commuters need is not the kind of regulation that holds back fare increases, but a recognition of the fact that mass transit needs funds."

MIT's Lang—and most other authorities—agree that the commuter fare structure is out of whack with what the traffic should bear. "When you subsidize commuter operations from general funds rather than by raising fares," Lang says, "you have a regressive income transfer from the average taxpayer to the fat cats in the suburbs."

A major problem, though, is that railroads like the LIRR and the Penn Central's New Haven division are asking for more money from fares now without being able to give the customers much—if anything—in return. "We can't cut fares, or even hold them at their present levels," Ronan says, "because we need every penny we can get to catch up on years of neglect. Almost all of our operating revenues go just to pay labor costs." The figure is 91.1 per cent for the LIRR, Ronan says, and he adds that on the New York subways, where operating expenses have been subsidized for years, the Transit Authority pays out $1.12 in wages for every dollar of revenue it receives.

Still, with all the problems, Ronan asserts that Long Island commuters have the best prospects for improved service quickly of anyone in the New York area. "Many of the 620 new cars on order have already been delivered," he says. "Rehabilitation of facilities is well under way. We're extending electrification. . . ."

The situation on the commuter railroads has become so visible that the key executives and politicians involved now find their careers dependent on what happens. . . .

Painful as it may be to contemplate for riders who know how bad the LIRR service can sometimes be, the Long Island is a pretty good sample of the wave of the future. Governor Rockefeller summed it up recently:

The important point is that while this railroad still suffers painful problems—delays, cancellations, and breakdowns—it is going through totally different kinds of problems today [from those under private ownership]. The pains the line suffered before were those experienced on the road to oblivion. The problems it is experiencing now are the growing pains that we encounter on the road to recovery. And there is a world of difference.

The difference, as Rockefeller sees it, is between "trying to keep a fifty-year-old commuter car from falling apart, and working the bugs out of a brand new car which will eventually replace ancient rolling stock."

RAILROADS AND A REGION: A CASE STUDY FROM NEW JERSEY [2]

Problems facing today's commuter railroads can be traced directly to the way the suburbs were settled.

North Jersey and Rockland County [New York] have a combined population today in excess of 5.3 million persons,

[2] From "Railroad Decline Compounds Area's Transportation Woes," by Edward J. Flynn, staff writer. Bergen County (New Jersey) *Record.* p 1+. S. 12, '67. Reprinted by permission.

yet the largest city in the region has less than 500,000 residents. Bergen County with a population nearing a million does not have a municipality with a population of 50,000.

Home development in the suburbs concentrated on single-family dwellings and earned the title bedroom communities. They focused on New York City—looking to it for employment, entertainment, education, culture, and marketing.

What tied the suburbs to the city was basically the commuter railroad. It took dad to work in the morning and brought him home at night, mother shopping in the afternoon, and the two out for a night in the city. All the while, the railroad rushed goods to the suburbs for the local stores, including coal—the main source of heat three decades ago. With a good passenger volume backed by a healthy freight operation, the railroads were making money.

Soon, however, the suburbs began spreading out and so did the commuter. As travel time became longer, commuters demanded express trains, stations closer together, and other features which only added to the railroads' expenses.

With the post-World War II building boom, the suburbs took a giant step, far outdistancing the railroad's existing lines. Then along came Detroit's assembly lines, producing cars by the mile, as Federal [and] state governments ran along paving the way with millions of highway construction dollars.

No longer did the commuter worry about catching the 8:10. He found freedom, convenience, and comfort in the family chariot turned commuter express. Still commuter trains operated, until other factors began pulling off riders and taking away the freight business.

Suburban shopping centers substituted for Manhattan's Fifth Avenue for most housewives . . . and television took care of Broadway, bringing the curtain down on late-night commuter trains.

Even Manhattan Island did not stand still for the suburban railroads. Business began moving uptown and to the
East Side, until commuters discovered trains didn't go where
they wanted them to. "For more than a hundred years the
railroads were oriented downtown, and commuter numbers
gradually went down as business moved uptown," recalls
George Eastland of the Erie-Lackawanna Railroad.

As a consequence of various shifts in locations of homes,
jobs, and department stores, the number of daily rail commuters from North Jersey and Rockland County totals about
70,000—half of what it was twenty years ago.

"Today we are left with only the rush-hour commuter
business and this has to carry the financial load for twenty-
four hours," says Eastland. Like any business, railroads determined they could not operate three or four hours a day
and make a profit.

Two years ago [Eastland says] the Erie-Lackawanna determined its so-called unavoidable cost at $9 million a year which in-
cluded taxes, depreciation, reinvestment, mortgages, and retire-
ment of facilities.

We went to the legislature, commuter groups, and service
clubs and told every one what we were going to do. We hoped
enough people would be interested to get action on the state level.
Nothing happened so we went to the Public Utilities Commission
with a request to discontinue all passenger service, and were allowed to discontinue half.

What has happened to the Erie-Lackawanna is typical of
other railroads in the area. Where they have not gone out
of business or declared bankruptcy, they have been forced
to either eliminate certain lines altogether or to curtail service on them.

In recent years, no less than four major and two smaller
commuter lines have been abandoned in the Bergen-Passaic-
Rockland area. The Erie-Lackawanna alone folded two of
its main branches, the Northern Branch which handled commuters in East Bergen, Northern Valley commuters in Bergen County and residents in eastern Rockland County, and

the Newark Branch, which connected Passaic County and Newark by rail.

A railroad which folded its commuter service completely was the New York, Susquehanna & Western, looked upon by many as having been probably the best commuter line in the metropolitan area.

How does a commuter railroad with that type of reputation go out of business? The Susquehanna had diesel engines, air-conditioned, self-propelled individual commuter cars, and the line ran through the heart of Passaic and Bergen County with stops in Paterson and Hackensack. For ten years, the Susquehanna petitioned and was denied a request to discontinue commuter service. Then one day in June of 1966, conductors informed homebound commuters there would be no trains the next morning.

Says Susquehanna President Irving Maidman, "The line lost at least $5 million and probably $7 million in the ten years of operation. The railroad couldn't earn money and there's no reason why private industry should subsidize a commuter operation." Maidman contends the line was capable of carrying three thousand commuters a day and that when it finally abandoned service it carried only a few hundred daily.

There is some disagreement, however, as to which came first—the commuter's abandoning the railroad, or the railroad's abandoning the commuter.

Frank E. Tilley, Jr., of Wyckoff, chairman of the Bergen County Board of Public Transportation, says bluntly:

The Susquehanna sabotaged the passenger service by cutting service, running trains late, and increasing fares.

Patronage went down [he continues] in direct proportion to reduction in service. When it had 30 trains a day it was carrying 3,000 passengers; when it cut it to two trains a day it had only 200 passengers.

Commuter rail service is looked upon by many railroad men as an inherent deficit operation. Only the morning and evening rush-hour trains carry anywhere near sufficient passenger volumes to sustain service. Off-peak service is a money loser and the rush-hour patronage cannot support the operation.

There is also another problem. As long as commuter service loses money, or just barely shows a profit, the owners are reluctant to invest in costly new equipment—even if it might bring back some lost patronage.

As a result most commuter railroad cars are dirty, without air conditioning, and old. The newest Erie-Lackawanna train, for example, is more than thirty years old.

> The rolling stock is not in good shape [admits Eastland]. We're not proud of it; it's old and the users deserve better equipment.

> We can't afford it, and we can't ask the board of directors for money. They wouldn't give to a business which has been losing money at an alarming rate. We feel it's the state's obligation. It's a public service, and we can't raise the fares to meet the cost or we would be driving away passengers.

New Jersey, as well as other states, has been subsidizing commuter rail operations.

> Faced with continuing pressure from the railroads to discontinue an unprofitable operation [says former New Jersey Governor Richard J. Hughes] we have been engaged in, and will continue, a program of millions of dollars in state subsidies and capital improvements to preserve this essential service.

For the fiscal year . . . [1968] New Jersey . . . [gave] commuter railroads $9.4 million in subsidy. Of this the Erie-Lackawanna, which operates rail service throughout Bergen, Passaic, and Rockland, will receive $4.2 million to maintain its present service. The state is also putting up an additional $1.8 million, which will be matched by Federal funds, to purchase seventeen air-conditioned coaches and two diesel engines. . . .

Many transportation observers contend, however, that state subsidy is at best a patchwork approach, and that what is really needed is an entire new transportation outfit. . . .

Whether or not continuing doses of state subsidy can save a sick rail commuter operation remains to be seen, but there is widespread agreement among transportation experts that it cannot be allowed to die. The reason is that the transportation balance today in the metropolitan region is so delicate the disappearance of the railroad would cause chaos on roads leading to Manhattan.

EASY RIDE ON A PHILADELPHIA TRANSIT LINE [3]

There's a mass transit system . . . [in Philadelphia] that is disproving one of the most cherished axioms of modern American life—that man can't be divorced from his automobile.

A high-speed transit system that went into service here a year ago yesterday is regularly drawing more than 40 per cent of its passengers from among people who formerly drove to work.

The popular line—which runs the 14.4 miles between downtown Philadelphia and suburban Lindenwold, New Jersey, in 22 minutes—is the first suburban commuter system built from the ground up to benefit from the advances made in the last fifteen years in automation, electronics and light-weight materials.

Carlos C. Villarreal, administrator of the Department of Transportation's Urban Mass Transportation Administration, said this about the system:

The Lindenwold Line has shown dramatically that an efficient public transportation system that has speed, runs on time and has clean equipment will attract a growing ridership by affording the motorist a choice. It is also an example of how the implementation of existing technology can provide immediate benefits to public transportation.

Officials of the Delaware River Port Authority, which runs the line, say it shows that modern technology can create

[3] From article by Robert Lindsey. New York *Times*. p 39+. F. 16, '70. © 1970 by The New York Times Company. Reprinted by permission.

an attractive, successful—and perhaps even a profitable—rapid transit system as long as it is freed from the railroad industry's traditional labor restrictions.

The system also has provided the country's best example so far of how a governmental agency can use profits from auto traffic—in this case, bridge tolls—to subsidize mass transportation and take motorists off choked city streets. . . .

Although it may be too soon to conclude that the concepts proved here will work elsewhere, the system so far is clearly a success.

Its passenger volume has increased monthly since it opened—to a current daily level of thirty thousand riders. It has eased congestion on roads paralleling the line and has accelerated the suburbanization of a grassy, lightly populated stretch of communities southeast of Philadelphia.

"My house has gone up in value $8,000 since they put in the high-speed line," a middle-aged insurance executive said recently as he sat in a deep, high-backed seat on one of the silver-skinned Lindenwold trains. While he spoke, the train . . . built by the Budd Company, accelerated gently up to seventy-five miles an hour.

Florence Schuck, a secretary riding to her job in Philadelphia, said:

"It used to take me an hour to drive in to work, sometimes an hour and a quarter. Now it takes me only twenty-two minutes. It's really a wonderful way to go to work."

Except for a barely audible whine in the train's electric motor and a distant hiss of air outside, the car was nearly silent as it glided smoothly over seamless welded rail. There were no bounces, jerking or clicking.

Irvin Shoemaker, a lawyer commuting from Lindenwold to Camden, New Jersey, said:

"I don't think I'd ever want to drive again. With the parking problem at Camden, it was getting impossible to take your car. I really didn't realize how good public transportation could be."

According to a recent poll by the Delaware River Port Authority, 40 per cent of the transit line passengers had commuted regularly before the line was built.

Twelve per cent used cars when they traveled over the route previously, but they were not regular commuters. This group—primarily young, unmarried girls—got jobs in Philadelphia and at other points along the line after the line went into service.

The rest of the riders either had used buses or trains on short segments of the route, or a combination of private and public transportation. . . .

Although the service lost $700,000 in its first year, when patronage was light at first, officials expect to make a $15,000 "operating profit" this year.

This profit would be the difference between fare income and expenses—principally salaries and electricity. It does not include amortization of the construction costs, which is being absorbed by revenue from bridge tolls.

The transit line is operated by the Port Authority Transit Corporation, a subsidiary of the Delaware River Port Authority. To pay for the $94 million transit system, the Port Authority doubled tolls to 50 cents on its two other principal properties—the Ben Franklin Bridge, over the Delaware between Philadelphia and Camden, and the Walt Whitman Bridge, between South Philadelphia and Gloucester City, New Jersey.

The transit link was built along the rights of way of two older lines—a deteriorated, thirty-four-year-old Port Authority rail line over the Franklin Bridge that was carrying about eight thousand riders daily between Philadelphia and Camden and the Pennsylvania-Reading Seashore Line between Camden and Lindenwold.

The line employs 210 persons, or the equivalent of about one employee for every 145 daily riders, a measure of efficiency that Port Authority officials here contend is by far the lowest in the world. One official, who asked not to be identified, said:

> We've automated just about everything we could. The low labor cost is the one reason we have a chance of going in the black.
>
> But if we tried to use the same equipment with the kind of labor "manning" contracts some of the railroad unions require, or if we were an existing railroad and tried to introduce new automated equipment over a union contract, we couldn't possibly do it. I think it's pretty clear: To make a go of it in this business now, you've got to start from scratch.

The advantages of an automated system can be seen in comparing it with a suburban run of the Long Island Rail Road.

The Lindenwold system can run a train with six cars, carrying about five hundred passengers, and pay the salary of only one on-board employee.

On the Long Island line, a train with six cars would generally have four on-board employees—an engineer and three trainmen to collect the fares. Manpower requirements are negotiated by the railroad and the United Transportation Union.

Fare Structure

How the labor-savings pay off is evident in the fare structures. The Long Island charges $1.20 for a 14.5-mile, one-way trip between Manhattan and Bayside, Long Island. On the Lindenwold Line, a trip of a comparable length costs 60 cents.

To visitors, the most striking aspect of the Lindenwold Line is its high degree of automation.

Passengers deposit coins in a machine at each station and receive a ticket about the size of a playing card. On the back, the ticket is coated with brown metal oxide that is similar to the coating of magnetic tape.

They insert the tickets into a turnstile-like gate. Within a second, electronic sensors scan the tickets, confirm them if they are valid, return them and open the gate. At the passengers' destination a similar machine confirms that the proper fare was paid and keeps the tickets.

The fare is 30 to 60 cents, depending on the distance traveled. Trains run every 4 minutes during rush-hours and every 12 minutes during mid-week.

The stations are spacious, with low, clean lines and a conspicuous absence of attendants. But each station is watched by at least one television camera that is monitored twenty-four hours a day from a central control station.

Security units are dispatched to the station if vandalism is observed. When a passenger has trouble with the automated fare system, the transit employee watching the TV screens can tell the passenger how to use the system by talking over a special telephone line that links the monitoring room with each station.

Each train has one crewman, a motorman who pushes only two buttons: one that closes the door and another that starts the train rolling down the track. Unless he has to stop in an emergency, the motorman does nothing else; the rest of the run is controlled automatically.

The train is accelerated, slowed up on curves, braked and stopped automatically at each of the twelve stations on the route by electrical signals transmitted to the train through rails and wayside markers.

"It's like a kid's supersized electric train run by remote control," a Port Authority official remarked.

BUSES ARE POPULAR BUT NOT PROFITABLE [4]

Private automobiles travel on the same rubber fiber over the same asphalt and concrete carpets thereby gaining the title of true competitor with buses—the backbone of mass transportation west of the Hudson River.

The fastest and most convenient means of travel in the tricounty Bergen-Passaic-Rockland area continues to be the automobile. In Passaic County, 80 per cent of all travel is done by car; in Bergen it's 90 per cent; and it's even higher in Rockland.

[4] From "Commuter Buses Run at a Deficit," by Edward J. Flynn, staff writer. Bergen County (New Jersey) *Record.* p 1+. S. 13, '67. Reprinted by permission.

The impact of this is seen every day. Stand virtually any-where during the rush hour and watch the traffic heading in all directions—Palisades Interstate Parkway at 8 o'clock in the morning, Broadway in Paterson at 4:30 in the afternoon, or even the intersection of Routes 4 and 17 on a Saturday. The scene is the same—miles of red tail lights inching along.

Just how much the suburban family has come to rely on the private car can be seen in Bergen County, for example. Bergen's population by the next census is expected to reach 1.05 million, exceeding Essex as the most populous county in New Jersey. It reflects a Bergen population increase of about 33 per cent since 1960. However, in a comparable ten-year period—1955-65—the number of cars registered in Bergen rose approximately 50 per cent to 374,156.

Knowing the tremendous percentage increases in passen-ger car registrations in the tricounty area, it would seem to follow that the number of commuters using buses and trains is also increasing. Not so. In the past twenty years, commuter rail patrons have been cut in half to approximately seventy thousand in New Jersey, while in the past dozen years the number of bus riders has remained the same.

The sharp drop in commuter rail passengers is under-standable. The railroads have been on the verge of financial disaster for years. As a result, they could not invest in new equipment and in many cases were forced to curtail or abandon service completely.

But the same is not true of a majority of the bus com-panies. Bus officials have tried to compete with the private automobile for business. Buses have been air-conditioned and made more roomy, schedule-frequency increased, more ve-hicles purchased to cut down the number of rush-hour standees, and express-service inaugurated on many lines.

"Passenger totals have remained about the same since 1954, despite the fact that the company is running more daily trips than in past years, and buses are also bigger with in-creased seating capacities," says Virden Rittgers of New Milford, general traffic manager of Rockland Coaches Inc. (Red and Tan Lines) .

Red and Tan is typical of the area's commuter bus service. Its daily passenger count in 1954 was approximately 24,600; today, it's about a hundred less. Inter-City, which recently filed a declaration of bankruptcy, has carried about 26,000 daily commuters for the past ten years.

Red and Tan handles the bulk of the commuter bus business between New York City and Rockland County and also the northeast section of Bergen County. Inter-City is one of the biggest haulers serving the heart of Passaic County and south, central and northwest Bergen County.

The biggest problem of these bus companies, the same as for the commuter railroads, is caused by the commuter morning and afternoon rush hour. Inter-City and Red and Tan officials estimate 90 per cent of their business comes from the peak hours, taking commuters into and out of Manhattan.

This presents a special headache to the bus business. "It costs the company more to provide rush-hour service," says Rittgers, "than the company receives in fares. Commuters are a money-losing proposition year in and year out." Rittgers estimates that for every 100 buses the company purchases (cost: $45,000 to $48,000 per bus), 75 are needed exclusively for the rush hour. In addition to the initial cost of these vehicles, companies must contend with the usual problems of maintenance and upkeep, along with special problems of ample garaging facilities and the need for extra drivers.

The one-way nature of the commuter business—getting the commuter into . . . [New York] City in the morning and taking him home at night—causes what is known in bus parlance as deadheading. For example, five buses leave from Ridgewood or Nyack between 7:30 and 8 in the morning bound for mid-Manhattan. Only one . . . is needed to handle travelers leaving mid-Manhattan for Ridgewood or Nyack. The other four return empty—deadhead back, and the rush hour is over before they can make another run into the city.

Driver workshifts, because of the short duration of the rush hour and the relative absence of reverse passengers, also present a problem. This means that for every four drivers needed to handle rush-hour volumes, only one is needed for regular-service runs. A bus company, according to Rittgers, must manipulate its drivers and buses to meet the peak commuter rushes.

Red and Tan handles this by having its regular drivers work the rush hours with some slight overlapping to cover the midday routes. The company also employs split-shift drivers, those who can make a trip into the City early in the morning and return in time to make another half-trip, starting at a point closer in. The same driver reverses this in the afternoon. There are also single-trip drivers, who make only a morning or afternoon trip, and who can fill in on vacations or be used for charter-bus service.

Why then do bus companies invest so heavily in equipment and manpower to serve a commuter operation which loses money?

The Red and Tan, for example, depends upon its charter service for a financial profit at the end of the year, according to Rittgers. Bus companies must keep up their commuter operations—even at a loss—or face loss of franchise which entitles them to operate in the highly-competitive charter business. At least on charter runs, profits can be determined in advance, using equipment already owned, and unlike commuter business, they can refuse the contract.

Whether bus companies will continue to vie for charter operations, or whether they will stand in line behind the railroads waiting for state subsidy, or whether they will be forced out of business by their commuter operations remains to be seen.

But as Rittgers says: "If the commuter wants a dollar's worth of transportation which costs $1.50 or $2 to provide—above what he's willing to pay in fares—the money will have to come from somewhere."

Critical of Service

Yet to many commuters, bus service is synonymous with waiting in inclement weather for buses that never seem on time, getting to work and home late, and always being faced with fare increases.

Time is the most important factor in the life of the commuter, especially for those who have migrated from the close-in core area to the thinly populated suburbs. Time and distance are almost interchangeable to the commuter, and he will choose that mode of transportation which is fastest, regardless of cost.

Many residents of western Rockland and northern Bergen County can get into New York City faster by bus than their neighbors living closer to the city. The reason . . . is express bus service which has been instituted on a number of routes. . . .

Buses are plagued with the same traffic problems as the private car. The situation becomes more critical the closer the traffic is to Manhattan. "Our big complaint," says Howard Edmonds, Inter-City's general manager "is that traffic is so bad in the afternoon that we can't get buses back into midtown to get more commuters out."

Inter-City's patronage is 90 per cent commuter rush-hour business and 95 per cent of it comes from Bergen and Passaic residents. The volume is so concentrated, especially in the afternoon, that almost every bus leaving the Port of New York Authority's Midtown terminal carries standees. Inter-City's Route 30 buses which serve Paterson commuters, for example, leave at two or three minute intervals in the afternoon with standing-room-only calls.

The situation for the area's bus commuters becomes intolerable in bad weather or [when there are] highway traffic accidents which delay buses. Either or both in the afternoon cause commuters to queue nervously and impatiently in lines extending farther than a football field.

"All we need is a wrapup on Route 3," says Edmonds, "and there's nothing you can do about it, unless there is some way of detouring around the accident which is almost impossible with no alternate roads."

Bus companies look to governmental and planning agencies for highway and traffic-control improvements that could speed commuter service. But their voices are neither loud nor persistent.

Highway lanes reserved for commuter buses during peak hours could expedite traffic flow, Edmonds allows, "But bus companies never made such a request probably because—although such a proposal would benefit the public—there still would be a certain amount of resentment."

Such a proposal has been endorsed by Roger H. Gilman, the Port Authority's director of planning and development, who told a Hackensack audience . . . , "On the basis of test runs, we believe there is an excellent opportunity to speed up bus travel, by designating as an exclusive bus lane in the morning rush hours, the innermost westbound lanes of the helix from the Lincoln Tunnel through the Union City cut to the Jersey Meadows."

Park-and-Ride

Still another proposal put forth to lure the commuter out of his car calls for park-and-ride facilities located along major expressways and highways, similar to the Lincoln Tunnel facility in Secaucus. The difference is that they would be located farther from the central core, thus relieving close-in traffic congestion. It is similar to proposals . . . to increase commuter rail service. Such an interlacing system, however, would require acres of land for parking, in addition to the construction of comfortable bus shelters.

There also have been a number of less spectacular and less costly proposals which, if put into effect, could speed commuter bus service appreciably. They include more realistic speed limits on major arteries served by buses, rush-hour parking restrictions on local streets used by buses, additional one-way streets, wider street corners which would allow buses more maneuverability, and synchronized traffic-light control.

All of these, plus more and better roads, are needed to get the commuter out of his car and onto some form of mass transportation. The alternative—get behind the wheel of the car, get in line, and wait.

NEW SYSTEMS FOR SAN FRANCISCO AND WASHINGTON [5]

The first trains on the $1.3 billion, seventy-five-mile rapid transit system now under construction . . . [in San Francisco] will not run until sometime in 1971 but there is already talk of expanding its network. The officials who run BART (the Bay Area Rapid Transit system) don't like to discuss it publicly—"We've got troubles enough as it is," one of them remarked. But it is clear that the pressure to expand the system will become irresistible almost as soon as it goes into service.

One of the reasons is that BART, as it is planned now, cannot fulfill the goal of reducing San Francisco's traffic congestion. Another is that areas around the Bay which are not on the system currently being built are beginning to realize what they are missing.

BART lost its chance to make a substantial improvement in the automobile problem before it was born when two of its five proposed lines were eliminated. The geographic peculiarities of San Francisco funnel automobiles into the central city over two bridges—Bay and Golden Gate—and up the east and west sides of the peninsula on which it sits. BART will provide excellent service for many of those people who now cross the Bay Bridge and for some of those who come up the west side of the peninsula but it provides nothing at all in the other two corridors and surprisingly little in the central city itself.

[5] From "The Psychological Side of Rapid Transit," by James E. Clayton, a member of the editorial page staff. Washington Post. p B 6. F. 1, '70. Reprinted by permission.

One reason for this is that San Mateo County, which lies just south of San Francisco on the peninsula, opted out of the system in 1962 on the grounds that its taxpayers wouldn't get their money's worth. Marin County, which lies to the north across the Golden Gate, withdrew soon afterward, partly because of an engineering report that the bridge could not handle rapid transit trains and partly because San Mateo's withdrawal upset the financial balance. The service BART had proposed to provide those who live in the city of San Francisco was crippled by Marin's withdrawal.

As a result, BART won't provide service in the areas where it would have the cleanest shot at persuading commuters to switch from automobiles. The publicly owned bus line that operates in the two counties across the Bay where BART will operate now carries about half the commuter traffic.

Already, however, there is talk about giving the two missing lines back to BART. A good many San Mateo residents are unhappy with a situation that leaves them a choice between autos and the Southern Pacific Railroad's commuter service. And the residents of Marin County, where public transportation is a joke, have always wanted a BART line.

Interestingly enough, it may be the San Francisco airport that forces BART to expand. The airport will not be connected to the rapid transit system when it opens because it is on the unbuilt San Mateo leg. But the Oakland airport, almost directly across the Bay, is close to a BART station and its operators are considering a shuttle-bus service like that in Boston. If this happens, the Oakland airport will be considerably closer in travel time, particularly in rush hour, from downtown San Francisco than the city's own airport. Given . . . [Civil Aeronautics Board] interest in spreading flights among airports, many passengers, particularly businessmen on short flights, may end up going to Oakland.

At the same time, communities such as San Jose, some forty miles away, are talking about linking up to BART. The idea of a rapid transit line that circles the southern half of San Francisco Bay utilizing the tube now under construction between San Francisco and Oakland, and perhaps a second that would connect the two airports, is not far-fetched.

Applying to the Washington area the factors that have led to this talk of expanding BART, it is not hard to foresee pressures before the end of the seventies to build extensions farther out into Virginia and Maryland. Nor is it hard to think of demands for short lines that connect suburban communities directly. The latter, however, is a function that Metro [Washington's new rapid transit system, now under construction] wants to assign to bus routes.

Fortunately, Metro does not have the missing segments of a basic system that BART has. Metro will go into all the suburban communities. But it will have the same problem of trying to wean customers away from their automobiles. Most of those who have studied BART believe the keys to success in this effort are an adequate system of feeder buses, no competition (or very little) from buses, and the creation of a psychology that riding rapid transit is the thing to do. Vital to rapid transit success, of course, are such things as the speed, quality and frequency of service and reasonable fares but the general assumption is that both BART and Metro will have few problems with these.

BART does have a problem with bus competition and feeder service since the cross-bay bus line is regarded rather highly. . . . Its operators have indicated no great willingness to go through the massive restructuring of bus routes that is needed, although this may well be part of a negotiating stance since the problem of transfers has not been solved. Nor have they indicated a desire to terminate their buses on the Oakland side of the Bay Bridge, thus keeping them off of San Francisco's streets, although this, too, may be negotiable.

Metro will have the same kind of problem in Washington unless it ends up owning the bus lines, as it well may. Even if it does, however, the juggling of bus routes will be enormously complex since most bus lines now run into the center like spokes on a wheel and with Metro in operation they should run in concentric circles fanning out from Metro stations.

The other prerequisite of success—adjusting the psychology of an area from riding in cars to riding in trains—has no easy handles either. San Francisco has one advantage in that its public transportation system is considerably better than Washington's. But no one . . . [in San Francisco] is sure how you go about making subway riding *the* thing to do, as it has become in Montreal. Perhaps it happens automatically through the allure of newness and speed. If that doesn't work, perhaps it can be helped along by drastically raising all-day parking rates downtown. But one way or another, this attitude is the crucial element in making a rapid-transit system work and San Francisco will have had some experience with it before Metro arrives on the Washington scene.

YES, THERE IS A FINE SUBWAY SOMEWHERE . . . [6]

The marble floors, rich carvings, and fine architecture of Mexico City's new subway bear a closer resemblance to an Aztec temple, or to the handsome National Museum of Anthropology, than to a rapid-transit system. While only the first of three lines has been put into service—the complete twenty-six-mile system will be ready in a year—it is already apparent that the subway, with its varied and inventive use of space, materials, and color, will be better looking than the much-celebrated systems in Moscow and Montreal.

Efficient, clean, and quiet, El Metro uses rubber-tired rolling stock imported from France, and other Parisian features such as platform gates to prevent latecomers from rushing at trains. The French equipment was financed with a $130 million loan from the Banque Nationale de Paris, which helps pay the otherwise prohibitive (for Mexico) esti-

[6] Article, "Mexico's Subway Is for Viewing," by Anthony F. W. Liversidge, an associate editor of *Fortune. Fortune.* 81:105-10. D. '69. Reprinted from the December 1969 issue of *Fortune* Magazine by special permission; © 1969 Time Inc.

mated total cost of $300 million. That cost, though, comes to less per mile than the subway in Montreal. And the Mexican builders emphatically declare that the artistic adornments did not add significantly to costs.

Such was the interest in the Metro that before it opened Mexicans stood over the ventilation gratings hoping for a glimpse of trains. But a more pressing reason than civic pride lent urgency to the project. The Aztecs who founded Mexico City never invented the wheel, but wheels jam the streets today. Millions of riders pour daily into the Zócalo, the central square. Long queues form at taxi stands, and rush-hour passengers cling for dear life as they hang out of the doors of buses they have waited an hour to board. And at 7,350 feet, the internal-combustion engine works inefficiently, causing smog.

Besides filling a clear need, the Metro is yielding rich archaeological treasure as a fringe benefit. Several thousand relics of the Aztec age have been unearthed, including the pyramid-shaped altar of Tocititlan, now the centerpiece of Pino Suárez station. Richer finds are expected as the second line is dug through the Zócalo, originally the Aztec ceremonial center whose pyramid temple and palace of Moctezuma so impressed Cortés. An Aztec stone calendar, like one in the museum, is known to lie along the new line's path. The booty carried by Spaniards who drowned attempting to escape the city with Cortés in 1520 may be found, too, as well as the rubble of the city they later sacked.

Push From a Prodigy

Building a subway in Mexico's capital is something of a technical feat. Liable to earthquakes, much of the city is built on and sinking into the still-waterlogged bed of a lake. To meet those difficulties, a cut-and-cover technique, floating a box-like structure just below the surface, was worked out by Ingenieros Civiles Asociados (ICA), the country's largest construction company, whose subsidiary, Ingeniería de Sistemas de Transporte Metropolitano, is building the Metro.

The prime mover behind the boldly conceived project is, in fact, the remarkable founder and chairman of ICA, Bernardo Quintana Arrioja, fifty. A prodigy of a businessman, the robust Quintana has the drive and imagination that largely account for the subway's splendid conception. Quintana started ICA when he was twenty-eight, forming a group of fellow engineers to build a public housing project, something he now calls "ladies' work." Today ICA, with sales of $220 million, is the biggest private enterprise in Mexico and has built most of the country's largest construction projects.

The one-peso (8 cents) ticket is expensive for many in this city of economic extremes. But the line is already carrying half a million passengers a day. The Mexicans have so far justified the faith of the designers that the fine finish, like the flowers that have been planted around the city in recent years, would be treated with respect, and not defaced or spat on. The prevailing attitudes seem, rather, to be pride, delight, and even awe. But the subway is not for sleeping; it is closed from one till five in the morning.

With the subway in service, streetcars are being phased out. But Mexico City is growing so rapidly that two more lines will soon be needed. No doubt these can be made handsome, too. As Bernardo Quintana says, "It costs so little to make a place beautiful. Modernity and progresss can very well be harmonized with tradition and beauty."

IV. ARE PASSENGER TRAINS OBSOLETE?

EDITOR'S INTRODUCTION

No area of transportation has suffered such a precipitous decline as intercity passenger service. Critics charge that railroad managements have deliberately driven passengers away with poor schedules, bad service, and dirty trains. But the railroads can show an all but unmarred record of financial loss on passenger service to back their requests to drop more trains from service.

What may be evolving is a system where there are few long-haul passenger trains, but more high-speed short-distance runs between nearby cities. An example is the Metroliner between New York City and Washington, where popular airplane service has added to airborne congestion. Trains could ease the aerial jam-up without much loss of time to travelers.

The first article in the section, from *Time,* levels the charge that passengers are being driven away from trains. Next, from the *Wall Street Journal,* a piece explains what happens when a railroad management goes before the Interstate Commerce Commission to request that a run be dropped.

Next, the highly successful system of Metroliner trains between Washington and New York City is analyzed by a consultant who had predicted that it would never attract enough riders. The last selection in the section, from *U.S. News & World Report* is a roundup of proposed Federal legislation to revitalize rail travel, including the Railpax bill approved by Congress in October 1970.

THE UNLOVED PASSENGER [1]

Unlike airlines, which promise to make the going great, and bus lines, which urge travelers to leave the driving to them, U.S. railroads, have increasingly been able to fend off passengers with shrinking schedules and slovenly service. Now both the public and the Government are fighting back.

Consumer crusader Ralph Nader charged last week that railroading "is the only industry I know of where a company has made toilet maintenance part of its cost-cutting program." In an angry demand for Government action, Nader continued: "The railroads have tried to make toilets so dirty that people just won't use them. That is part of the total effort to drive passengers away."

The Justice Department decided that the abrupt cancellation of an Omaha-to-Billings, Montana, train last summer at remote Hemingford, Nebraska, was outrageous enough to file criminal charges against two Burlington Lines executives. When an expiring court injunction permitted abandonment of the service, they had the train flagged down in mid-run, stranding several irate passengers. The executives were accused of failing to provide service for tickets previously sold; if convicted, they would face fines of up to $5,000.

The Interstate Commerce Commission refused to allow the Louisville & Nashville to scrap the only remaining train between St. Louis and Atlanta. If patronage was poor, the ICC said, it was due "in no small measure to a marked deterioration in service." Neither food nor beverage vending machines, noted the indignant commission, were provided on the 609-mile run.

In an industry that lost $200 million on passenger service in 1968, horror stories of unconscionable service and rachitic equipment are a valuable asset. They help trains to become "underpatronized"—and therefore eligible for cancellation under ICC rules. There were 1,400 intercity passenger trains in 1958; now there are only 488. Every road in the United

[1] Article in *Time*. 95:48. Ja. 5, '70. Reprinted by permission from *Time*, The Weekly Newsmagazine; Copyright Time Inc., 1970.

States is out to emulate the half a dozen carriers, from the Boston and Maine to the Frisco, that have succeeded in eliminating passenger business entirely. President Louis W. Menk of Northern Pacific might have been speaking for the industry in November when he told a House committee: "I make no mistake about it. I want out."

The 61-27 Limited

To speed the way, the railroads have adopted a number of plans calculated to make the going miserable. Penn Central has walled up the main entrance of its Detroit terminal and removed the baggage lockers inside. A sign in a Union Pacific train advises passengers that "on days livestock is to be carried, Train 82 runs about a half-hour later than the schedule shows." The Southern Pacific, the nation's most profitable railroad, has employed classic tactics to depopularize the once elegant Los Angeles-to-New Orleans Sunset. Phone calls for departure and arrival information go unanswered, and printed schedules are hard to find. Anyone venturesome enough to get aboard can expect forty-four hours in a coach seat (no sleepers) and meals from a bank of vending machines.

The railroads practice all sorts of tricks with timetables to discourage traffic. The Chesapeake and Ohio schedules its trains between Detroit and Grand Rapids to arrive after 2 A.M. The Southern Pacific's Lark reaches Los Angeles from San Francisco thirty-five minutes too late to connect with the eastbound Super Chief and twenty minutes after the last train to San Diego. Passengers on the Baltimore & Ohio's night train from Washington to Detroit are put off at Fostoria, Ohio, at 5:30 A.M. and loaded aboard buses for the last leg of the trip. Then there is the nostalgia-tinged "last run," epitomized by the New York Central two years ago when, with much hoopla, it sadly announced the end of the Twentieth Century Limited between New York and Chicago. Actually, the train still runs, complete with Pullmans, dining and lounge cars, but it is now known merely as Train 61-27.

Not Just Buffs

There is ample evidence, experts say, that fast, modern rail service could fill a vital need between at least seventy-five U.S. city-pairs 200-300 miles apart. The Penn Central's high-speed Washington-New York Metroliner has been operating with 75 per cent of its seats filled, despite bugs in the computerized reservations system. For years the Seaboard Coast Line has been running New York-Miami trains that are popular, comfortable and profitable. The Florida Special, which cleared $300,000 last season, is booked for weeks in advance by passengers who enjoy such amenities as color TV and a recreation car where airline-style "hostesses" put on fashion shows.

Such successes collide with the industry-fostered notion that passenger-service advocates are just sentimental buffs. In 1968, the railroads carried a substantial 92 million passengers, not counting commuters. Yet there is no denying one industry contention: the debt-laden railroads cannot afford costly but needed improvements.

Congressional Action

At present, the passenger's future is in the hands of Congress, which is considering a dozen bills to improve railroad service. The main features of most of them are contained in a bill being prepared by the Senate Commerce Committee. At a cost of up to $445 million over the next four years, the bill would provide funds for new equipment, subsidies for money-losing operations, and an office within the Department of Transportation to manage basic passenger services—in effect, a quasi-nationalized system. The plan is anathema to most proponents of private enterprise; yet, as even the railroads concede, it seems to be the only way that the United States can regain the quality of railroad passenger service that Europe and Japan still enjoy.

SHALL THIS TRAIN BE DISCONTINUED? [2]

Gary Balliett, a social studies supervisor for a suburban school system, rides Penn Central trains between New York and the Midwest a couple of times a year to attend educators' meetings. He complains that the railroad runs the trains slower every year and doesn't publicize available service anymore. Moreover, he says, buying tickets is an "ordeal," passenger car air conditioners and water fountains don't work and frequent schedule changes leave him "discouraged."

Nevertheless, Mr. Balliett, testifying here yesterday at an Interstate Commerce Commission hearing on a Penn Central application to cut back service, said that he still preferred to ride the train rather than fly or take the bus to the conferences. Riding the train gives him a chance to relax and get some work done on the trip, he said.

Though the number of train riders keeps going down every year, more people like Mr. Balliett are showing up at local hearings to protest proposals for taking off additional money-losing trains. Among their arguments: They need the trains to visit relatives, they don't have or don't like air and bus service, and they would ride trains more if they were cleaner and ran on time and the personnel were nicer.

The current [May 1970] Penn Central case seems certain to set a record for protester turnout. As part of a plan to halt all Penn Central passenger service west of Buffalo and Harrisburg, Pennsylvania, the road is currently seeking to drop thirty-four intercity trains. The most involved in any previous hearing on intercity service was six (though in 1965 the New Haven Railroad proposed in vain to drop 274 commuter trains at once).

The Penn Central hearings are to last two months, moving across New York State and on into New Jersey, Pennsylvania, Maryland, Massachusetts, Ohio, Indiana, Michigan,

[2] Article, "Passengers' Plaint: More People Protest Loss of Train Service, But Results Are Mixed," by Albert R. Karr, staff reporter. *Wall Street Journal.* p 1+. My. 12, '70. Reprinted by permission.

Kentucky, Missouri and Illinois. The nation's railroad map would be left with "gaping holes" if all thirty-four trains were dropped, a passenger group remarks.

Hearings like these would no longer be necessary if the railroad-rescue bill that passed the Senate last week becomes law, as is deemed likely. A semipublic corporation, starting with $40 million of Federal money and selling shares to the public and to member railroads for cash or equipment, would take over intercity passenger service as of next March 1 [1971].

In advance, Transportation Secretary John Volpe would decide which trains were essential; the others could be discontinued without ICC hearings. A nonmember railroad would have to keep its essential trains running at least until 1975, as would the corporation. The proposal has wide backing in the Nixon Administration, Congress, the industry, railroad labor and passenger groups. [Railpax, as the corporation is known, was approved by Congress in October 1970.—Ed.]

Meantime, public interest in local "train-off" hearings climbs. Usually, it's greatest in small communities, where it's a big event when the hearing lawyers come to town. Recently in Dillon, Montana (population 3,690), 45 people turned out to oppose a still-pending Union Pacific attempt to drop a Butte-Salt Lake City train.

In big cities passenger service is less involved with civic pride, and fewer complainers show up. At yesterday's Penn Central hearing here about fifteen witnesses protested the railroad's bid to discontinue ten trains running between New York and the cities of Pittsburgh, Chicago and St. Louis. But even that number was greater than usual for a big city; Edmund Fritz, the ICC examiner who conducted the hearing, says the last such proceeding he held in New York drew only a third as many witnesses.

About 450 intercity passenger trains are running today, down from about 1,500 a decade ago. Every year more towns find themselves without service. Alarmed state and local officials are working harder to develop a good showing at

ICC hearings. Some state regulatory agencies now hold advance hearings of their own to line up witnesses. And past successes at keeping trains running have spurred the trend.

A Forum for Grumblers

Railroad officials, predictably, aren't pleased at all. "The hearings merely provide a forum for dissatisfied people to complain all out of proportion about the railroads," insists an attorney for one big road. Yet, he adds sadly, the ICC gives "some weight" to their complaints.

Not always enough weight, says Anthony Haswell, chairman of the Washington-based National Association of Railroad Passengers. The Commission, in making its decision, also takes into account such factors as the railroad's financial losses, and sometimes, according to Mr. Haswell, a train is allowed to die even when public witnesses have made "a strong case" for its survival.

Participants in train-off cases say a profusion of testimony about poor service can have its influence. Implicitly, the ICC acknowledges this.

It heard from 353 witnesses, including members of Congress, governors, state legislators, local government officials and union officers, when the Northern Pacific (now part of the Burlington Northern system) asked permission to discontinue its Mainstreeter between St. Paul and Seattle. In subsequently rejecting the plea, the commission cited the hearing testimony as evidence that the train had been downgraded by ending through "slumber-coach" service, side-tracking the Mainstreeter to let freight go by and neglecting to provide baggage attendants.

Other times the outcome is different. Last July a hearing was held in Grand Junction, Colorado, on the request of the Denver & Rio Grande Western to drop its Denver-Salt Lake segment of the California Zephyr. A highlight was testimony by John F. Emerson, a Union Carbide Corporation division manager. Partly because of the derailment of another train and a mudslide, he said, his daughter and her two young children spent twenty-one hours in the coach section between Denver and Grand Junction. She couldn't get pillows, blankets or milk for the nine-month-old baby, nor persuade any crewmen to bring her checked baggage from the adjoining car so she could get diapers. The ICC allowed reduction of the Zephyr from daily service to thrice-weekly.

When the question arises of need for trains, reasons vary widely. College students often stress that trains are the only way for them to travel between school and home, on weekends or vacation. One man said he wanted the train to keep running because he liked to hear the whistle.

A persistent need is expressed by funeral directors, who say alternate means of shipping bodies for burial are too expensive (planes) or in bad taste (trucks). Grand Junction undertaker Paul Martin, noting that many people are afraid to fly, told the hearing examiner that "when it comes to transporting their loved ones from one part of the country to another, they naturally have the same fears there." A small-town hearing had to be recessed for a couple of hours so that an undertaker-witness could direct a funeral—and the other witnesses could attend it.

While attorneys for state agencies or passenger groups do their best to wring from witnesses reasons for keeping the train running, railroad lawyers counter by trying to demolish the testimony. A typical ploy is to ask a person pleading for a train how long it has been since he rode one. "It's surprising how often the person protesting has never been on the train," says one veteran railroad lawyer. In a case involving a Baltimore & Ohio train between Chicago and Akron, the ICC took pains to note that only 30 of the 64 persons testifying at nine hearings actually ride trains.

WHY THE METROLINER IS SUCCEEDING [3]

Consultants' forecasts tend to get shelved in corporate libraries never to be heard from again, unless, of course, the

[3] From "About Those Metroliners: A Consultant Admits (Happily) That He Was Wrong," by William E. Griswold, associate, Systems Analysis and Research Corp. *Railway Age*. 167:30-1. D. 15, '69. Reprinted by permission.

forecast turns out to be correct. In this happy event, few consultants let modesty stand in the way of an opportunity to point out the accuracy of their predictions. Less frequently, however, is the consultant pleased to announce that his forecast has proven incorrect.

In May 1968, *Railway Age* published my article "Who Will Ride These Trains?" in which I forecast that passenger response to the TurboTrain and Metroliner services would be minimal. An increase in demand of less than 10 per cent was predicted.

In the case of Metroliner service, this forecast was clearly too conservative. In the first nine months since Metroliner service was introduced, rail travel between New York and Washington increased by 72 per cent over the previous year. The factor which apparently explains why passenger response to the Metroliner service has been so much greater than anticipated is a factor not normally included in "accepted" transportation forecasting methodology: anxiety.

Conventional travel demand forecasting techniques usually take into account four major characteristics. These are, in order of importance: frequency, speed, cost and accessibility. (Some researchers also include "comfort" but this is a very difficult concept to measure. Comfort is apparently not a factor in the modal choice decision, provided all modes offer a "reasonable" level of comfort. Comfort appears to be a factor only when all other factors are substantially equal, as when the traveler is choosing among carriers of the same mode). Measured in terms of these four factors, the present Metroliner service appears to rank a poor second. One would not expect considerable diversion from other modes.

As this is published, 6 Metroliner round trips are operated daily between New York and Washington. For the first nine months of 1969, when a 72 per cent increase in demand was generated, only 3 round trips were operated. In contrast, the airlines offer upwards of 50 daily round trips between New York and Washington. On the basis of schedule frequency,

Metroliner service was not at all competitive with the service offered by the airlines.

Speed is the next most important consideration. Measuring elapsed travel time from downtown, an airline trip from downtown Washington to downtown New York requires from 2 to 2½ hours, assuming no major delays en route due to air traffic congestion. Current Metroliner schedules require from 2½ to 3 hours for the downtown to downtown trip. So, in spite of the considerable reduction in rail travel time which Metroliner offers, the rail traveler still has to allow about 30 minutes longer on a New York-Washington trip than does the airline passenger. In terms of speed, Metroliner service is not yet competitive with airline service.

Measured in terms of cost, Metroliner service fares a good deal better, as the following table shows:

Mode of Travel	One Way Fares	
	June 1969	December 1969
Airline—Coach	$19.95	$23.10
Metroliner—First Class	21.65	21.65
Metroliner—Coach	13.75	15.75

A traveler accustomed to flying coach between New York and Washington could travel first class on Metroliner for about the same cost. Since fares were increased in October 1969, Metroliner first class is actually cheaper than the air shuttle fare.

Alternatively, a traveler paying the Metroliner coach fare can now save $7.35 each way, or $15 round trip, compared with the cost of flying. When the lower cost of taxi fares to and from the centrally located rail terminals is included in consideration, the overall cost of a round trip by Metroliner becomes about $25 less than an equivalent journey by air. Thus, depending on class of travel used, Metroliner is equal to or better than airline service in terms of cost.

In terms of accessibility, the fourth major factor to be considered, Metroliner again does not compare favorably with its competition. By accessibility is meant the ease with which a reservation can be made and a ticket obtained. Obviously, unless the passenger knows in advance that he is going to be able to obtain a seat, he is in most cases unwilling to set out. Recognizing this need as an essential element of travel marketing, airlines have developed fairly sophisticated computerized reservations systems which maintain an up-to-date record of seat availability for each flight. The Eastern Air Lines "Air Shuttle" service, as is well known, goes one step further by dispensing with ticketing procedures and guaranteeing a seat to all passengers who arrive on time, thereby eliminating the need for reservations and tickets. (To the experienced traveler this is a mixed blessing since the "extra section" departs up to one half hour later than the scheduled departure time.)

Seats on the Metroliner are by comparison relatively less accessible. Penn Central offers fewer downtown locations where a ticket can be obtained, and it is generally necessary for the traveler to make a special trip to the station a day or two in advance to pick up his ticket. The high average load factors being maintained by the Metroliner service, while indicative of its popularity, also have an adverse effect on seat availability. Probability analysis indicates that at the 75 per cent load factor which the Metroliners are averaging, one out of every two potential passengers who inquire will be told that a seat is unavailable. Under existing conditions the factor which will determine whether load factors will go any higher is not demand, but the ability of the reservations system to keep current on the availability of seats.

In October, when the number of daily Metroliner trips was doubled from three to six, some DOT [Department of Transportation] spokesmen were quoted as doubting whether such high load factors could be maintained in the face of such an increase in capacity. Preliminary results indicate that load factors under the new timetable are as high or higher than they were with three trains per day. The evidence is that the demand for intercity travel in the Corridor is so great that even hourly service will not make a significant dent in the total demand moving by all modes. Since better service stimulates even more demand, the last thing Metroliner management need be concerned about is overproduction.

In sum, Metroliner service compares favorably with air travel in terms of cost, but ranks unfavorably with respect to frequency, speed and accessibility. Since cost is relatively unimportant to the businessman traveler, why has Metroliner service proved to be so popular?

A possible factor which emerges from on-train interviews with passengers is that the Metroliner service generates less *anxiety* than does a comparable trip by air. This is not to say that businessmen are afraid to fly; on the contrary, flying is usually fun. But the process of completing a New York-Washington trip by air requires fairly continuous and active participation of the passenger, at least subconsciously.

First, there is the problem of finding a taxi, not an insignificant problem in New York. En route frequent reference to your wristwatch is needed to determine whether you will make it to the airport on time. Once there, you must wait in line and judge by the number of people ahead of you whether you will make the first section. (If you don't, the Metroliner would have been faster.) When you are settled in your seat, it is time to "fasten your seat belt and place your seat back in a full upright position." Then, as the plane taxis out to the runway, you count the number of planes in line ahead of you and calculate the approximate delay until takeoff. Seasoned "Air Shuttle" veterans can easily recall the remainder of the ritual. Only during the brief thirty-minute cruise between takeoff and landing does the average passenger find himself free of travel responsibilities and able to concentrate his attentions elsewhere.

In contrast, the Metroliner passenger need actively participate in the progress of his journey only for a few minutes at the beginning and end of his trip. One of the appeals of

Metroliner service which businessmen mention frequently is the fact that they can look forward to two *uninterrupted* hours en route when they can read a report or prepare for the day's meetings. Freedom from interruption is really another way of saying freedom from anxiety. So long as the train remains in motion, no active participation is required of the traveler.

For travelers who have switched to the Metroliner, relative or perceived speed appears to be more important than absolute speed. The freedom from en route delays and relative certainty of on-time arrival make Metroliner the preferred mode of travel.

Passenger response to the Metroliner service is all the more remarkable since it has been stimulated by a service which in terms of frequency, speed and accessibility is not yet competitive with airline service. What this suggests is that no new "space age" technology is required to accomplish a fairly dramatic reduction in airways congestion in the Northeast Corridor. If a 72 per cent increase in demand can be achieved on the basis of three trains per day, it seems apparent that a schedule offering departures every hour on the hour, with further gradual reductions in running time, and implementation of planned improvements in the reservations system, should result in a substantial diversion of present New York-Washington airline passengers to Metroliner service. It is beginning to look increasingly as though the solution to the "fourth airport" problem in New York will arrive by rail.

If passenger response to an hourly Metroliner service frequency between New York and Washington is as great as it appears that it will be, one inescapable conclusion is that similar service should be offered between New York and Boston, presumably via a new electrified right-of-way over an inland route through Connecticut.

WHAT'S BEING PLANNED TO SAVE RAIL TRAVEL [4]

A showdown is rapidly approaching on plans to save the vanishing passenger trains of this country.

The Senate Commerce Committee has one plan. The Nixon Administration is working on another. . . .

In short, there is now a feeling of urgency about the trains. . . .

In the past two decades, the amount of passenger service provided by the nation's railroads has declined by nearly two thirds.

Back in 1959, there were nearly 1,200 passenger trains running on regular schedules. Today there are fewer than 470. And the companies are seeking to discontinue 50 of these. Many of the remaining trains are on short commuter runs, some of them operating only because the states and cities are paying millions of dollars toward their costs. Trains for long trips are few and far between.

As things stand, the future holds only more of the same declining trend. The year 1970 had scarcely begun before the Erie-Lackawanna wrote an end to another of the nation's historic trains, the Phoebe Snow. The Erie now provides no rail passenger service between Chicago and the New York-Newark metropolitan area.

To go north to Maine today, you have to use a car or plane, unless you plan to hike the Appalachian Trail. The trains have stopped running. New Hampshire and Vermont no longer have rail connections.

There are no passenger trains from Chicago to southern Arizona, Pittsburgh to Cleveland, Atlanta to Chicago.

The last two trains giving sleeper service between Chicago and San Francisco—the California Zephyr and the City of San Francisco—will run no more, if the railroads have their way. They are being kept in operation only by orders of the Interstate Commerce Commission—orders that by law cannot be maintained indefinitely.

4 Reprinted from article in *U.S. News & World Report*. 68:58-9. Ja. 19, '70.

Freight Is First

The railroads' rush to drop so many trains reflects a desire to cut losses and concentrate on hauling freight, which is profitable. The industry's accounts, following ICC rules, indicate a loss of about 200 millions a year on the remaining passenger runs, when they are charged with a share of the overall cost of tracks, terminals, maintenance and administration.

A recent ICC study of eight major lines found that they were losing $118 million a year on passenger service, when only the costs that could be avoided by discontinuing the trains were counted.

These heavy losses and diminishing service form the backdrop for the new approaches being studied.

The plan pending in the Senate Commerce Committee calls for a Federal subsidy to cover 80 per cent of the losses a railroad sustains in operating a passenger train if the ICC rules that this train must be kept for the convenience of the public.

This formula is similar to one in use in Canada. It relies on the companies to continue to manage the business, but with the Government footing the bill.

The subsidy idea receives strong backing from some railroads, notably the Penn Central, which alone provides about 35 per cent of the nation's passenger service and figures a saving of more than $60 million a year if these operations were discontinued. The Penn Central lost more than $40 million on all of its rail business in the first nine months of this year, but some of its passenger runs are so important that it has little hope of being allowed to abandon them.

A number of other railroads seem to believe that, unless the Government will cover 100 per cent of the deficit, they will do better with the present law, gradually sloughing off their passenger traffic until their losses become negligible. These companies note, also, that the Senate bill contains only

$60 million a year—not nearly enough to offset even 80 per cent of the money dropped by the entire railroad industry in carrying passengers.

Still other lines say they want nothing to do with a Federal subsidy.

Thus, the industry appears to be split on that approach.

Railpax

Interest is shifting to a different plan, favored by the Department of Transportation—a plan to set up a nation-wide corporation known as Railpax to handle all passenger service.

The railroads would provide some of the company's working capital, based on the amount of money they save when Railpax takes over financial responsibility for the trains. According to one formula, this contribution would be 50 per cent of their savings each year for three years.

In return, Railpax would pay the railroads a fee for hauling the trains and for the use of their equipment.

The big hope, as backers of this plan see it, is that Railpax would do a better job of managing the business than the industry is doing. It would alter fares, try out new or better services, and introduce new equipment, perhaps eventually invest in revolutionary trains with wholly new propulsion systems capable of speeds of 250 miles an hour.

What if, in spite of its efforts, Railpax lost money on some or all of its trains? It, too, could drop them—unless states and cities served by these losers were willing to make up the losses.

Some officials think Railpax might be able to save a good many trains that are threatened with oblivion. The Federal Railroad Administrator, Reginald N. Whitman, is only cautiously hopeful, however. He told lawmakers:

"It appears that any requirement for continued service lies essentially in a number of short-haul, high-density corridors, plus perhaps a skeletal long-distance service."

Another official questions whether Railpax would be able to extract much money from states and cities already hard-pressed to meet other needs.

Railpax, in short, seems to offer no ironclad assurance that the trains, many of them, will not stop running.

Why is there this seemingly insoluble problem?

Travelers and unions blame the industry. They say the companies skimp on equipment, upkeep and service and are, in fact, trying to discourage people from riding in order to make a case for discontinuing the trains. An ICC examiner scored the Southern Pacific on that very basis.

These critics say the Penn Central's new Metroliners, which are attracting many new customers to the railroad between New York and Washington, show what can be done if the companies will offer faster, more convenient service and get Government help. DOT is paying 13 million of the estimated 58-million-dollar cost of the Metroliners.

Labor Costs Blamed

It is the industry's contention that losses on trains are caused chiefly by high and rising labor costs on the one hand and diminishing passenger loads over which they have little control on the other.

The companies say—and DOT officials tend to agree with them—the Metroliner is a special case that may, at best, be duplicated in a few short corridors where there is an unusually heavy flow of travelers. Except for these situations and the commuter trains, the rail executives see no economical future for passenger business.

The industry claims to have spent more than $1.3 billion on new equipment between 1946 and 1958. Various lines tried out new types of trains, special reduced fares, modern food service, other innovations designed to please. Still, patronage dropped 50 per cent during that period, as more and more riders switched to roads and airways.

Said Mr. Whitman:

There is a general belief that poor quality of rail service and lack of interest on the part of the railroad industry was the main element that brought about the dismantling of a once massive rail passenger network. Such criticism may be justified in certain cases, but it is not the basic reason for the overall decline in intercity rail service.

Where once the businessman, vacationing family and occasional traveler had to go by train, the choice of rail today runs a poor third. The public wants the speed of air travel and the economy and flexibility of the private auto.

Actually, the problem of passenger losses seems almost worldwide. Experts say no national systems are making a profit on passengers. The New Tokaido Line in Japan is making money, but the Japanese National Railways system as a whole loses heavily and is thinking of abandoning 1,600 miles of lightly patronized passenger lines.

It is against this gloomy background that Congress and the Nixon Administration are approaching a decision on what, if anything, to do to save the trains.

[Congress approved the Railpax plan in October 1970. —Ed.]

V. AIR TRAVEL: THE PROBLEM IS SUCCESS

EDITOR'S INTRODUCTION

When we turn to consider the area of transportation by air, we find no story of declining traffic and decaying facilities. More passengers fly every year on newer, faster, better planes. But the rapid changes and growth in the airlines industry have created their own special galaxy of problems. Many of the difficulties are on the ground, where scarce land and neighbors' complaints are making airport expansion very difficult.

The first article in this section gives an overview of the airline picture today. The focus in this article from *Time* magazine is on the introduction of the new jumbo jets. Also mentioned is the argument over whether the supersonic jets now on the drawing boards should be built, or whether their noise and possible pollution outweigh their benefits.

Two following pieces, one from the *New Republic,* one from the *Saturday Review,* discuss the problems on the ground. Where can needed new airports be built? How can old ones be modified to serve jumbo planes? A final selection from *Saturday Review* considers some of the new smaller planes and helicopters that might serve some urban needs.

READY OR NOT, HERE COMES JUMBO [1]

The high white contrails of cruising jets are bright symbols of the promise and pleasures of air travel. When the big ships descend into sight and sound, their aspect alters. Their great engines foul the air with noise and noxious fumes; their proliferating numbers crowd the airways with danger-

[1] From article in *Time.* 95:52-6. Ja. 19, '70. Reprinted by permission from *Time,* The Weekly Newsmagazine; Copyright Time Inc., 1970.

ous traffic jams. Each new plane seems to bring more problems than the last. But the newest and largest product of
this technological age is built to a different pattern. The
Boeing 747, first of the generation of superjets that will dom-
inate the skies in the 1970s, is quieter and cleaner than its
predecessors. Its huge capacity will help airlines keep ahead
of their expanding roster of passengers. The new planes
should alleviate rather than increase the clutter aloft. In the
process they will bring new comfort, convenience and economies to ever greater numbers of travelers.

Boeing's 355-ton superjet is 231 feet 4 inches long—three
quarters the length of a football field, longer than the
Wright brothers' first flight. Its twenty-foot-wide cabin is
almost twice as broad as the largest passenger plane now in
service; it can be fitted with up to 490 seats. More like a small
cruise ship than any familiar aircraft, the big plane brings
to mind comedienne Bea Lillie's comment on the Queen
Elizabeth: "When does this place get to England?". . .

With their remarkable efficiency, . . . [the superjets] will
help hold fares down at a time when everything else is
going up.

For all such benefits, the superjets will create some giant
problems all their own. Airport managers nervously await
the great clots of passengers that will be disgorged from a
single flight. Practically no terminal is prepared. In the first
months of 747 service, baggage handling and ground transportation—already overstrained—may be utterly swamped.

Airline managers are equally concerned. The 747 is so
costly that its advent has plunged the industry deeply into
debt. When one line buys a new generation of aircraft, all
feel the urge to follow. At a time when profits are down,
credit is expensive and other costs are climbing, the airlines
feel that they have no choice but to order the 747s. So far,
twenty-eight of them in the United States and abroad have
ordered 186 of the superjets at around $23 million each.
That amounts to a capital outlay of $4.3 billion.

The initial cost is only the beginning of a new round of expensive investments that the superjets make necessary. Airlines must spend another $2 billion for new facilities and equipment in the next four years, including fifty-four-ton tractors to tow the big planes and new boarding ramps to lift passengers to doors that are seventeen feet off the ground.

The airline that will be first with the most 747s, and thus must cope with every one of the bumps in what airmen call a new plane's "learning curve," is Pan American. As if that were not enough, the company is already experiencing more than its share of turbulence. Last year [1969] it lost an estimated $23 million, $7 million in the month of November alone. It is getting much tougher competition from archrival Trans World Airlines on the North Atlantic route, and it faces a flock of new competitors on transpacific routes that it once all but monopolized. Now, with the 747, Pan Am is taking one of the larger risks in business history. It has committed $1 billion to buy thirty-three of the jumbo jets and create the facilities to handle them. The company is staking its corporate future on the big ship.

The man who must make the wager pay off is Najeeb Elias Halaby, fifty-four, Pan Am's new president and chief executive. Halaby has not yet had time to demonstrate that he can lead a losing airline back to solid profits, but he has sound credentials for that difficult job. Before he landed at Pan Am, he was in turn an outstanding pilot, a practicing lawyer, a corporate executive and an imaginative, activist chief of the Federal Aviation Administration. He also showed himself to be accomplished in personal public relations, seldom failing to remind audiences that he was President Kennedy's principal adviser in all aviation matters. Pilots who met him at the gossip sessions known as "hangar fly-ins" took to greeting him with the line: "Halaby thy name. Thy will be done, on earth and in the heavens."

One of Halaby's major assets is the fact that he probably knows more about the 747 than anyone outside of Boeing.

As FAA administrator, he framed many of the Government rules that will regulate the plane's flights. Last year, when reports filtered through the industry that the big ship was in trouble, Halaby went to Seattle to take the 747 on a test flight. Settling into the left-hand command seat, he piloted the plane through its paces for two hours, then gave a singularly satisfied description of its virtues.

You keep thinking that you have 17,000 pounds of thrust in four little levers [he said]. You've got your hands on a hurricane on the ground. You have to be careful, because the blast could blow in a hangar door. Another thing: you've got 355 tons of momentum when you're taxiing that machine, and you don't go charging around. So you have got to plan ahead while taxiing. But once it's airborne, it's absolutely superb.

Halaby took the 747 through high-altitude stalls and a series of landings and takeoffs. "You become integrated with the ship. That big fin and so much rudder contribute to stability and control." The plane was so bulky that he found that it seemed to dwarf the runway. Landing, he reported, was "like training for carrier landings." When he taxied back to the hangar, the feeling was "like docking a patrol boat— you've got to sail it in, and very carefully."

It's a confidence-building machine, straightforward and honest [adds Halaby with unbridled enthusiasm]. Once passengers get aboard, they will have such a feeling of space, of strength, yes, even security, that any early anxiety will disappear. It is going to be, for older people, like going back into an ocean liner. For the youngster, it is going to be a different kind of life in the sky, where he can move around, go up and down the deck, feel less inhibited and constrained than he was in previous airplanes.

Stepping into the 747's passenger cabin is indeed like walking onto the passenger deck of a luxury cruise ship. The aisles are wide, the walls nearly straight, and the ceiling an unconfining 8 feet high. Economy-class seats are 10 per cent wider than on an ordinary jet. Coats and carry-on baggage are stowed in large overhead storage compartments. The cockpit is in the prominent bulge atop the plane's front end, along with a surprisingly spacious bar and lounge for first-class passengers, reached by a winding staircase. On the main deck below, the cabin extends out into the nose of the aircraft. In the economy section—which is separated by galleys into cabins so large that TWA recently held a board meeting aloft—passengers sit nine abreast in rows of two, three and four, divided by two wide aisles. The total effect is of roomy comfort. In flight, the 747's heft helps to smooth out some turbulence but, as in every other airplane, passengers in the rear are subject to the most movement in bumpy air.

To many people, the sheer size of a superjet raises the horrifying image of a supercrash. The thought of as many as five hundred passengers and crew members going down at once seems too appalling to contemplate. Even so, actuaries in London, where most airline insurance is written, forecast three 747 crashes in the first eighteen months of service. Each accident would cost the insurers up to $65 million. Balanced against their projection is an actuarial fact: though 98 of the 3,012 jets that have gone into service in the past dozen years have been lost in accidents, air travel—measured on an aircraft-mile basis—is five times safer than it was a decade ago.

Moreover, judged by its extensive new equipment, the 747 ought to be the safest aircraft ever built. The superjet has three inertial-navigation systems—the same sort that has guided Apollo flights—lest one, or even two, should fail. There are two auto pilots instead of one, a redundant supply of communications gear and an advanced radar with a three-hundred-mile range. The 747 even has an automatic landing system designed to bring it safely to a runway in any weather without the touch of a pilot's hand.

Gaps on the Ground

As its biggest boosters are all too well aware, it is on the ground that 747 passengers will find what Halaby calls "a surface-transport gap, a hotel gap and a parking-lot gap." There is also that conspicuous airport gap. The 747 can land in the same length of runway as a 707, but its sheer size makes many other changes necessary. The only airport in the world that claims to be fully prepared for the 747 is Paris's Orly, which has already built one separate terminal and has another under way. By June, London's Heathrow will be the second adequately equipped airport, with an expanded terminal and twice as many customs officials. Tokyo's Haneda airport, probably the world's most crowded terminal, has made preparations only on paper, and no one knows how its thoroughgoing customs officers are going to handle the crush. JFK airport in New York will not be fully prepared until 1973.

Ground transportation of every variety is already overloaded. Authorities at Kennedy and other airports may eventually have to ban private cars altogether, allowing only buses and taxis to drive up to the terminals. New York's Metropolitan Transportation Authority plans a rail line on an unused right of way of the Long Island Rail Road between JFK and Penn Station to whisk passengers to midtown Manhattan in twenty minutes. But the first trains probably will not be ready until 1974.

Winning by Losing

Congress is moving belatedly to supply funds to equip the nation's airways and airports for the superjet age, and most of the load will fall squarely on the air traveler. By spring Congress is likely to pass legislation to raise nearly $1.8 billion a year in new revenues. The ticket tax on domestic flights will rise from 5 per cent to 8 per cent, and there will be a new "head tax" of $3 on passengers flying overseas and a 2 per cent tax on air freight. The money will be used to improve airways by adding new navigation and communications aids: airports will also be improved.

Perhaps the most surprising fact about the 747 is that the plane that promises to accomplish so much actually began its existence as a loser. In 1964, Defense Secretary Robert McNamara ordered a competition for a giant military transport and an advanced jet engine to power it. Lockheed and

General Electric won the plane-and-engine competition, and their entry became the C-5A. The two losers, Boeing and Pratt & Whitney, were eager to find a market for their rejected designs. Boeing's chief, William Allen, decided to risk what turned out to be $1 billion in turning the military reject into a commercial success. Pan American's founder, Juan Trippe, who had ordered the first 707s a decade before, was still in command. He backed Allen by placing the first order for twenty-five of the 747s and taking an option for more.

To get production under way, Boeing had to construct one of the world's largest buildings—a plant covering 42.8 acres at Everett, Washington. Inside that vast space, the engineers encountered vast problems. The aircraft's weight grew by fifteen tons from its projected 340 tons, and Pratt & Whitney had to rush development of a still more powerful engine. Because it burns its fuel more efficiently than other engines, the 747 is virtually free of the greasy smoke that trails ordinary jets on takeoff like ink from a frightened squid. Its engine is only half as loud as a 707's, though the difference will be less noticeable during takeoffs than landings. The new engine was not put into production as fast as the plane. Boeing last week [mid-January 1970] had fifteen expensive airframes sitting powerless outside its plant.

Once attached, the new engines brought another serious difficulty. As the turbines thrust forward in flight, the rear casing was bent one twentieth of an inch out of shape, letting jet gases leak around the turbine. Result: the engines lost some of their power and fuel consumption rose a costly 5 per cent. Pratt & Whitney finally found a solution by modifying the mounting, in effect adding an extra strut to carry the thrust. The new part will not be ready until the first thirty aircraft have been built.

Early design difficulties are inherent in building any plane, and the 747's major troubles now seem to be overcome. . . . Recalling a recent conversation with Pan Am's best-known director, Charles Lindbergh, Halaby says: "Slim Lindbergh and I were sitting in the 747, and we decided to

list the greatest civil air transports of all time. We picked
the German JU-52, and DC-3, and DC-6, the 707 family of
jets, and DC-8s—and this airplane, the 747." . . . Halaby expects that Pan Am's lead with the 747 will help the line to
turn a quick if temporary profit this year; 1971 will be a
tough year because by then so many competitors will have
their own fleets of superjets. . . .

Squalls of Competition

Pan Am is not alone in feeling the profit crunch that,
in the year ending last September 30 [1969], held U.S. airlines' investment return to 3.7 per cent, down from 9.5
per cent in 1967. "Nobody can make money in the . . . airline
business these days," says C. R. Smith, chairman of American
Airlines until 1968. "The economics represents sheer hell.
Practically everybody is in trouble."

The economics of aviation was little better eleven years
ago, when the 707s first flew into service. Then, airline executives wondered how they could possibly fill the expensive
new jets or pay for them in a time of economic slowdown,
slackening passenger growth, and steeply diving profits. For
several years, the planes flew with too many empty seats.
Not until 1963-64 did they achieve their full potential. Then
the jets became the airlines' biggest moneymakers ever; airmen called them "the flying cash registers." Now Halaby
and other industry chiefs hope that history will repeat itself,
and the chances are that it will. The CAB [Civil Aeronautics
Board] predicts that passenger travel on U.S. lines will more
than double by 1980. The notable economies of the 747
should enable airlines to wring more profit out of that increase. The jumbo jet can be particularly productive as an
all-cargo carrier, and could cut the cost of sending a ton of
air freight from Dallas to Tokyo, for example, from $340
at present to $135.

The immediate outlook, however, is for a few years of
costly overcapacity. Pan Am will have 362 seats to fill per
747 flight, and TWA has ordered fifteen superjets with

342 seats each. Even Ireland's little Aer Lingus has asked for two 400-seat versions for jampacked all-economy flights between Dublin and New York, presumably relying on Irish loyalty and cut-price deals to fill them. Besides overcapacity, the 747 will bring higher operating costs. Pan Am's senior pilots will get paid $58,000 a year to fly it; airport authorities are asking for triple the landing fees that airlines pay for a 707.

Meanwhile, the industry continues to be troubled by fare-cutting competition from unscheduled airlines. So-called "supplemental" lines carry passengers at fares far below airline rates, passing on to their customers the economies that result from having every flight a 100 per cent full charter. During Halaby's term as FAA administrator, Washington set rigid new rules for the proliferating—and sometimes unreliable—supplementals. The Government weeded out the weaker ones, reducing their number to about a dozen. In the years since, they have burgeoned again, cutting deeply into the scheduled-airline business.

The scheduled lines' answer has been to offer "bulk" fares. The lines sell wholesale blocks of tickets to travel agents, who retail the seats for as little as $175 for a New York-London round trip (provided that the passenger also pays $100 in advance for meals and services at his destination). Another bargain is the new "group inclusive tour," which reflects the power of foreign government-owned airlines in the International Air Transport Association. International fares are now designed to encourage tourists to make fairly long visits to individual foreign countries in which they will presumably spend more money. As a result, tour fares, which include round-trip ticket, hotel room, some meals and theatre tickets, can supply a remarkably inexpensive two-week stay in many a European city.

The 747 may allow even more attractive package deals. Regular fares, however, are unlikely to be cut; businessmen and others who stay abroad for fewer than fourteen days will continue to pay relatively high prices for airline tickets.

On domestic runs, U.S. airlines were granted two increases totaling more than 10 per cent last year, and some lines are now rallying lobbyists to press for another boost, on the order of 3 per cent.

Executives of the supplemental lines argue that they serve the public interest by helping to reduce fares. They are calling for looser regulation, and are asking for State Department assistance in negotiating new landing rights abroad. In rebuttal, Halaby makes the point that scheduled airlines are already tightly regulated and overwhelmed by a surfeit of competition. As he puts it: "We should abandon the recent trend toward multiplication of carriers and the inevitable addition of deficits."

In an effort to reduce extreme competition and improve profits, many airlines are talking merger. The United States hardly seems in need of a score of trunk and regional airlines. American Airlines has discussed merger with Western; ailing Eastern, admits President Floyd Hall, is "studying every other U.S. carrier" as a possible merger partner. TWA has considered both National and Northeast. Pan Am executives have held informal talks with American, Eastern, Delta and Continental.

Pan Am could compete on better terms if it were allowed to feed into its overseas routes from inland gateways like St. Louis and Dallas, or permitted to acquire a medium-sized domestic line to give it a home base matching TWA's. The Justice Department may well fight tie-ups between any two of the very biggest lines, but there is little doubt that the Administration will permit some mergers. Most airline executives agree that there will be fewer carriers surviving by the end of the 1970s.

Debate on the SST

The financial benefits of togetherness will be all the more important because the lines will have to raise so many billions to pay for the 747 and other superjets in the future. Next summer, test pilots are scheduled to take up the first of the huge, three-engine "air buses"—McDonnell Douglas'

DC-10 and Lockheed's 1011. Both are expected to enter service by 1972 and carry 250 to 350 passengers in comfort comparable to that of a 747. So far, 382 of the air buses have been ordered. Originally designed for shorter-range routes than the 747, the trijets are now being offered in stretched intercontinental versions as the two manufacturers compete for orders. In the continuing competition of bigness, Boeing has designed a 747 that can carry up to 750 passengers. Eventually, the jumbo jets are likely to reach capacities of 1,000 and 2,000.

Congress [has] voted $86 million—of an eventual $1 billion or more—to underwrite development of an aircraft of less obvious benefit: Boeing's supersonic transport, or SST. It is the U.S. answer to the British-French Concorde and Russia's TU-144. The SST will, as Halaby says, "turn the Atlantic into a river and the Pacific into a lake." But it will be much less economic than the 747, and passengers will have to pay premium fares.

The SST has divided the industry. Halaby, who as FAA administrator supervised the original competition for an SST design, says that he is an unabashed "supersonophile." He seems confident that the plane's problems can be solved. Pan Am Director Lindbergh has questioned the SST as a potential despoiler of the environment. Unless there is a breakthrough in design, the SST will spread a sonic boom beneath its path up to fifty miles wide. "Slim and I are in constructive debate on the SST," says Halaby. "I'm for it and he's not."

So far, the supersonophiles are winning, and the U.S. SST is likely to be in service by the late 1970s or early 1980s. The lines are expected to have a broad mix of planes and fares: premium prices on the SST, regular tariffs on jumbo jets, somewhat lower fares on older jets. By then, the problems of air travel will have multiplied, creating an even greater need for improved control of airspace, more airports, better ground transportation and bigger, more efficient terminals. Halaby worries because public investment in such facilities has always lagged five to ten years behind technological innovation. As the 747 takes to the air, its first and most important lesson is that the disparity must be corrected.

AIRPORTS FOR JUMBO JETS [2]

The only airport in the world really prepared for the 747 is Orly in Paris. Admittedly this situation both pleases and confounds the airlines people. A notable foot-dragger at such international events as world's fairs, France began to cope with the jumbo jet problem two years ago, now has one satellite terminal ready for joint use by Pan Am and TWA, and will have a second satellite ready by . . . May [1970] in time for the arrival of the first Air France 747. Telescoping bridges, twice as wide and six feet higher than those used for the 707, are already in place, and a moving sidewalk will connect the jumbo jet spurs to the main airport.

Dr. Joseph Smith, a psychologist who deals in motivational research for airlines among his other customers, says:

I submit if we put all our energy and muscle to work I firmly believe we can deal with the problem of discharging twice as many passengers from an airplane. My God, we just put a man on the moon, and this is really not that complex either from a technological view, or a practical view, or an application view. It's a lickable problem. What it requires is the recognition of its importance and the willingness to commit the effort against it.

Not many cities have displayed either recognition or much willingness to meet the arrival of the jumbos with suitable space. An informal survey of airports conducted by *Saturday Review* showed these plans and accomplishments:

Frankfurt, Germany, . . . [unwrapped] the first part of its elegant $178 million airport . . . [in January 1970], with more than ample room to dock a score of 747s or even bigger craft. A $27 million, high-speed luggage conveyor capable of handling sixteen thousand pieces an hour and three moving

[2] Excerpt from "Will It Be the Soaring Seventies?" by Horace Sutton, associate editor, and David Butwin, travel editor. *Saturday Review*. 53:34-7. Ja. 3, '70. Copyright 1969 Saturday Review, Inc. Reprinted by permission.

sidewalks to rush passengers from terminal to apron are being made. Hangar No. 5, biggest in the world, could hold the Eiffel Tower prostrate, but, more important, six 747s.

Washington's Dulles is one of the few airports designed from the start to handle outsize craft and needs only minor modifications, namely the stretching of pavement, to give the 747 a little more room to maneuver. Under consideration are curbside conveyors for baggage check-in and prechecking of luggage at the downtown terminal. Congress, meanwhile, is looking at a rapid transit service to Dulles.

San Francisco International is adding a third passenger terminal building, while the two existing ones are expanded and the parking garage is enlarged from 2,700 to 8,000 stalls. A freeway now under construction, when finished, will alleviate traffic congestion for a few more years.

Boston's Logan Airport opened a new terminal building [in 1969], and two more will be completed by 1973 at a cost of $100 million.

Los Angeles International's new streamlined clearance system will stall passengers coming in from foreign locations for no more than two minutes at a booth representing public health, immigration and naturalization, customs, and agriculture, another 8.5 minutes if a second stop for baggage inspection is ordered. Two 747 gates will soon be ready. A pair of new freeways and three entrances to the airport through tunnels beneath runways and taxiways are planned.

Cleveland's Hopkins International passengers like the year-old rapid rail service that does the eleven-mile run from downtown to airport in twenty minutes. When Cleveland joined Tokyo and Brussels as the only cities linked to airport by fast rail service, it anticipated two thousand riders a day. It has doubled that figure consistently.

Philadelphia International will have its $200 million expansion completed by the nation's bicentennial in 1976. If a driver parks his car in an airport lot, he'll be no more than one thousand feet from the plane he's about to board.

Beyond the deep-rooted problem of terminal facilities are the corollary difficulties of moving even more hordes of people and their baggage through such presently overcrowded airports as Chicago's O'Hare and New York's John F. Kennedy—and, once that is accomplished, of transporting them from terminal to town. American Airlines, for instance, has in readiness a sophisticated, computerized baggage system called Docutel, on which it has been working for three years. Here is how American's Jack Mullins explains it:

If you were a passenger and you arrived at JFK, a Skycap or our agent would take your bag and give you a check. He would then place this bag into a container which is like a tub. He would type into a computer where that bag is to go, by just hitting a few digits. Magnetic impulse carries it to a sorting area. On arrival at destination it is held until you call for it. Your baggage claim check, when inserted into a slot, will call up the bag, delivering it to a choice of locations: the parking lot, at the curb, at an inner-line connecting point.

Even allowing for the times the computer sends your bag to Anchorage, while the airline deposits you in Tulsa, the system is not only ingenious, but it is definitely apace of our technological times. The trouble is that it is expensive, and American is reluctant to install it at Kennedy Airport because the entire roadway and parking system will have to be changed, and *that* project hasn't even been begun yet. American, to use it as an example, will have its first 747 in June [1970], but its baggage system, at the most optimistic estimate, will not be in operation until January 1972.

Howard B. Johnson, the thirty-seven-year-old heir to the ice cream and motor lodge business, who is expanding his company in enormous strides to keep up with the rush of the seventies, has dire views of the days ahead.

Now just for example [he says], you realize that there are already 35,000 to 40,000 people working at Kennedy right now, and they're talking about getting up to 100,000 people working at the site. And on Saturday and Sunday they have traffic jams just from the people coming out to visit Kennedy. Well, you're going to have to spend billions of dollars on the airports just to get the people to the planes. The hordes are going to bury us.

It is quite true that passengers have missed their planes both at Los Angeles International Airport and at Kennedy because they couldn't get through the traffic jams inside the airport grounds. Passengers aboard the proving run of the first Boeing 747 may have made it from Seattle in four hours and five minutes, but they were stalled in traffic for half an hour just trying to *get out* of the airport. The rail link from New York City, which has been contemplated for years—a line already goes out to the nearby Aqueduct race track—was approved only . . . [in 1969]. Nine miles of track is needed to connect the fast rail service with New York City's Pennsylvania Station, but even if work begins tomorrow, the line won't be operational until late in 1972, barring delays.

Even considering the necessity of such a rail line to ease the automobile traffic, the project has been meeting with the customary criticism from local residents whose cause is championed by politicking local statesmen who object . . . to "a low-flying railroad" speeding dangerously through residential areas merely for the benefit "of a few select Manhattan residents."

It is just the marshaling of such partisan local objection that has beaten down the possibility of a fourth jetport in the New York area, which had once been proposed for Morristown and later Solberg, New Jersey . . . , Somers, New York, and the abandoned air base at Newburgh, New York, about which Governor Rockefeller himself recently expressed some doubts. Says [Najeeb] Halaby [president of Pan American World Airways],

> The most serious problem we have is in airports and airport access. For ten years we tried to get the jetport sited and nobody wanted it, and yet everybody wants the results of it. People are believing that airports are a menace rather than a facility. They think of another runway at the airport not in terms of providing more convenience to more people but in terms of providing more noise to a handful of neighbors. They're not thinking of this train to Kennedy as a way to permit perhaps forty million people instead of sixteen to use Kennedy—the greatest good for the greatest number. They're thinking, well, maybe if that train goes by my apart-

ment it will wake the child, and they're having more success in blocking transportation improvement.

All manner of imaginative ideas have been broached, including an offshore airport in the New York area similar in concept to, but even bolder than, Kai Tak in Hong Kong and Faaa in Tahiti, both of which were built into the sea.

One plan suggested by designer Lawrence Lerner would place a nine-mile-long structure in the ocean bottom five miles off New York that would be capable of handling ships as well as planes. Hydrofoils and perhaps Hovercraft would provide some of the linkage to the mainland even as these new marine devices are being suggested for such water-girt cities as San Francisco and New York.

THE JETPORT TANGLE [3]

The fantastic growth of the $6 billion airlines industry has thrown a scare into those who have to worry about jet-ports. Airfields which only a few years ago were considered adequate until the seventies have already become bottle-necks. The industry's ultimate problem may not be how to fly better, but rather where to put the things that must rest on dirt.

In the New York metropolitan area the problem is espe-cially acute. The Port of New York Authority, the bistate agency that operates the airports, has for years been urging a start on a fourth jetport to supplement Kennedy, LaGuardia and Newark. Last March, Austin J. Tobin, the Authority's executive director, called the jetport problem frustrating. According to the New York *Times,* he fears that likely limita-tions on travel for businessmen and movement of air cargo will divert business to other centers; he also fears that the potential for "physical disorder," including air collisions, may become "frightening." The Authority's wish for a new

[3] From article by Walter Pitkin, Jr., writer and teacher at New York Uni-versity. *New Republic.* 156:11-12. My. 27, '67. Reprinted by Permission of *The New Republic,* © 1967, Harrison-Blaine of New Jersey, Inc.

jetport, which may cost $350 million, is shared by the Federal Aviation Agency, New York Senator [Jacob] Javits, [former] New Jersey Governor [Richard J.] Hughes and others. Nelson Rockefeller has urged two more jetports, for a total of five.

The trouble all along has been to agree upon even one site. Most of the suggested places turn out to be aeronautical duds, because of air-traffic conflicts with planes headed for existing jetports. Other sites are in hilly country and would be too costly to develop, or are too far away. Still others that might otherwise do are soon surrounded by mobs of noise-hating, placard-waving citizens shouting, "Never, never!" As New York's jetports handle roughly one eighth of the nation's air passenger volume, the final choice will have important consequences for the country.

Last year [1966], 28.5 million passengers used the three jetports, up 10 per cent from 1965. . . . For the years 1970, 1975 and 1980, the Port Authority foresees air passenger demand at 40 million, 53 million and 65 million, respectively. My own estimates for the first two years run higher.

But landings and takeoffs, rather than passenger flow, create the pressure for another airport. Last year, plane movements at the three jetports came to 853,000, up 11 per cent; a similar increase is likely this year.

Scheduled airlines account for only part of this jetport activity; nonairline traffic is also flying high. A large part of aviation using New York's jetports has been air taxis and executive aircraft. In February [1967], these two types of small plane, together with individually owned aircraft, accounted for one quarter of all landings and takeoffs. It is predicted that by 1970, nonairline traffic will account for 37 per cent of total movements at the jetports.

Easy flow of air passengers is important to the local economy. For example, it is good for the city that apparel buyers from all over the country can get to it as easily and swiftly as they still can, despite mounting delays. Nevertheless, a stiff price is being asked, in dollars and in sacrifice of whatever peace and tranquillity remain, and it seems high time that people begin to ask how many monstrous jetports Megalopolis should agree to accept.

Jetports eat up huge amounts of land; about ten thousand acres each, which is almost four fifths the area of Manhattan Island. The new Dallas-Fort Worth jetport is gobbling up 21,000 acres. "Invest in land," reads a sign outside a Cress-kill, New Jersey, real estate office, "they aren't making it any more." In fast-growing Megalopolis, people are going to need all the land there is to live on, or perhaps just to play on or look at. They also want to be spared aircraft noise, as the following headlines from the New York *Times* and New York *Post* show: "Plan Is Proposed on Airport Noise"; "Jet Noise at LaGuardia Drawing New Protests."

[Former] Governor Hughes has been subjected to political pressures from thousands of people in Hunterdon and Morris counties who want no part of a jetport. Rockefeller's efforts to clear the way for a jetport at Calverton, seventy miles out on Long Island, have run into protests from area residents and politicians. It seems that any new metropolitan jetport would be rejected if it were put to the vote of the 200,000 people living nearest it. Noise is not the only nuisance: there is the burnt kerosene odor around busy jetports. Last May, [New York] Mayor [John] Lindsay's Task Force on Air Pollution identified one of the sources of the "poisons and dirt" in New York's air as "the emanation from approximately 400,000 takeoff or landing operations of jet aircraft at New York airports each year." Nobody likes that, but how else than by building still another jetport can New York (and perhaps other cities) adequately provide for fast-growing air commerce? The answer is to make more efficient use of present jet facilities, by refusing jetport access to all classes of nonairline aviation. To soften the blow, the rule might first apply to only two, then three peak hours daily. The final stage would be complete exclusion.

The capacity of an airport is measured by its ability to handle rush-hour movements when visibility is limited and

Instrument Flight Rules (IFR) are in force. Under IFR, aircraft must be spaced farther apart than they may be when visual reference is permitted. Port Authority figures show that the critical IFR capacity for the three jetports in the entire period 1970-1980 will be stable at 173 per hour. Against this capacity, the Authority's predicted peak-hour aircraft movement demand, for airliners and all-cargo planes only, is 144 in 1970, only 141 in 1975, and 157 in 1980. Even in this last year, therefore, the three jetports' excess IFR capacity should be on the order of sixteen per hour.

Why the downturn in peak-hour airline movement demand from 1970, and the modest increase afterward even as passenger traffic zooms? In part, the phenomenon is explained by the much greater number of seats in "stretcher" planes already beginning to come into use. In addition, some rescheduling of outbound flights, away from rush hours, will result from the introduction of the French, British and American supersonics in the seventies.

Thus it appears that the sole reason for a fourth jetport before the eighties is to provide big airport conveniences for the users of the fashionable air taxis and executive aircraft.

A limited class uses nonairline aviation: politicians, aviation executives, bankers, heads and subheads of major corporations. Governor Rockefeller, who uses a five-passenger family-owned jet to stump around New York State, has included in his transportation program a scheme for three new general aviation airports in nearby Suffolk, Westchester, and Rockland counties. Together with similar existing facilities, and others that are proposed, these should allow for substantial growth of nonairline flying. But for the convenience and safety of the vast majority of airplane users it would be a mistake if exclusion of small planes from the jetports (which Rockefeller does not propose) were to await completion of even one of the new mini airports. That there may be some hazard in the mixing of general aviation and airlines is suggested by the fatal collision of a private plane and an airliner on the runways at LaGuardia on May 2 [1967].

The Regional Plan Association, while sympathetic to the claims of general aviation, has a firm grasp of priorities for the metropolitan area. It says: "The public interest requires that both general aviation and airline flights be well accommodated. But when demand exceeds the availability of limited airport and air space near the center of the region, it is clear that priority must be given to the huge majority of air passengers traveling on airliners."

Last December, the Port Authority rejected diversion of general aviation, saying it had interviewed about nine thousand users of general aviation in 1965, and "no more than 15 per cent of the total general aviation operations would find it equally convenient to use other airport facilities." But we need to provide for the many, not the few. The more difficult problem for today and tomorrow is not air access, but ground access. It would make more sense if the Port Authority were to take the hundreds of millions of dollars that a jetport would cost, and spend them instead on ingenious ground access systems for the 65 million people a year who will want to use the airlines by 1980.

Suppose the Port Authority is wrong in its projections, and that the 65 million passengers turn out to be 75 million. A 1967 decision not to build a fourth jetport still would not have been a blunder, for there are other remedies that can be applied at any time. One would be to study and test regulatory and economic devices for spreading critical peak-hour plane movements into less crowded hours. On its shuttle runs on the New York-Boston and New York-Washington routes, Eastern Airlines has been experimenting with $2-plus differential fares that make it cheaper to fly in off-peak hours. Similar experiments on longer hauls, such as New York-Chicago and New York-California, where the dollar differentials could be greater, might succeed even if the Eastern tests proved inconclusive.

John R. Meyer, professor of economics at Harvard, recommends use of peak-hour surcharges on top of regular airport use fees. "The time has come to use this leverage to distribute airport use more evenly," he says. "This is at the heart of the doubts which some airline experts have about the urgent necessity of new major jetports. It will also restrict the growing volume of private air traffic and perhaps speed the creation of separate airfields for such private and executive transports."

A further step would be to cut out unnecessary airline flights, such as those to Philadelphia, which has excellent downtown-to-downtown train service to New York; then flights to such close-in cities as Boston, Providence, Baltimore and Washington can begin to be rationed. Flights to and from all these points within Megalopolis account for about a quarter of all airliner movements at New York jetports. It can even be argued that now is the time to start choking off such flights, to create pressure for a main-line railroad from Boston to Washington that is up to Japanese standards. [Penn Central's Metroliner is the first step in this direction. See "Why the Metroliner Is Succeeding," in Section IV, above.—Ed.]

A VOCABULARY FOR THE SEVENTIES [4]

Long before the current decade is halfway spent, the public will be required to know the rudiments of a new technical language about superjets, jumbo jets, supersonic aircraft, and, perhaps oddest of all, the appellations given to those aircraft that take off and land in bizarre ways. Jumbo jet is the term given to Boeing 747, the Lockheed L-1011, and the Douglas DC-10. A flying machine referred to as VTOL takes off and lands vertically. V/STOL can take off vertically, but, should a runway be available, it could fly off with more

[4] Excerpt from "Will It Be the Soaring Seventies?" by Horace Sutton, associate editor, and David Butwin, travel editor. *Saturday Review*. 53:37-8+. Ja. 3, '70. Copyright 1969 Saturday Review, Inc. Reprinted by permission.

people aided by a relatively short roll down the tarmac. STOL has no vertical capabilities; it uses a short distance in which to get off the ground.

V/STOLs and helicopters will figure prominently in managing airport transfers during the coming years. One version of the V/STOL (for vertical/short take-off and landing) has been developed by Textron's Bell Aerosystems Company of Buffalo. This weird bird . . . is powered by four propellers that look like electric fans. Pitched in the ordinary posture of propellers, they can drive the plane forward at more than 320 miles an hour. With the turboprop engines turned to a horizontal position, the plane can hover or descend like a helicopter. Ling-Temco-Vought, Hawker-Siddeley, Curtiss-Wright, and de Havilland of Canada are also developing V/STOL aircraft that would work well within such tight urban complexes as Boston, New York, and Washington, and also function as fast ferries from existing airports.

Najeeb Halaby [president of Pan American World Airways] says somewhat ruefully:

We could have had a STOL-port in operation along the North River [in New York City] this summer if we had not run into serious political problems. We had acquired an option on property at the foot of 59th Street at the Hudson River. We could have put on a Twin Otter twenty-two-seat operation toward the end of next year. But there were fears by some of the more militant neighborhood groups that, if you let in a little STOL, you'd get a huge STOL making a huge amount of noise.

Besides protest, Pan Am has also run into the tangle of jurisdictions, including the hard-nosed Port Authority, with the result that a STOLport in New York is now a good five years away. Charles Tillinghast, TWA's chairman and chief executive officer, says it will never be built because it is too noisy, potentially too pollutive, and would create more traffic problems. "Initially intriguing until one begins to think about the ground traffic problem that would be involved," is the way Tillinghast wrote it off.

Even the most casual observer might wonder, what with all our experience with helicopters in Vietnam, whether a civilian adaptation of a vertical take-off aircraft (or VTOL) might not emerge for civilian use.

Sikorsky Aircraft feels its spacious eighty-five-passenger helicopter, still on paper, can outdo the STOLs. Its thirty-seat choppers are operating in the Los Angeles and San Francisco areas and soon will return to New York skyways. Sikorsky's dream helicopter, the S65-200, would rise on a dime and cruise at 265 miles an hour.

Our aircraft [says Rick Hellyar, who heads the project at Sikorsky] is at home at the lower altitudes, and for good reason. We don't want to get up into that mess. When we're flying for just fifty-five minutes—the flight time between New York and Washington—we don't want to get up there where everybody else is.

Studying the market for a maxihelicopter, Sikorsky has met with better reception abroad; U.S. airlines tend to favor the STOL.

In Europe [says Hellyar] the cities are so much older, much more densely developed, they almost automatically have discounted any kind of STOL downtown service. There is simply not the room. Another reason is that rivers in Europe, famous as they are, aren't anywhere near the size of the Hudson. So there just isn't the maneuvering room a STOL would need.

Although Sikorsky has gotten its most favorable reactions in Europe, it also has a friend, or at least an ally, at Pan American. A vigorous, innovative airline, it is now hard pressed by foreign flag carriers. Its own routes, on which it has been dominant (California to Hawaii, for example), are now beset by competition from other American carriers. As a result, Pan Am, which had earned nearly $40 million for the first nine months of 1968, lost $4.5 million for the same period of 1969.

Sikorsky's Hellyar analyzes it this way:

To make things equal now, Pan Am has got to get into this country. They want domestic service. You've got to give them credit for bravery, because they're saying, "We'll tackle your toughest problem." Rather than, "Give us New York to Los Angeles where we can make a bundle," they say, "Give us the short-haul problem." They have made this position public. I suspect it's going to have a lot of political appeal. It means the Government has got to make an appointment and pour money into something. You can be sure Pan Am will fight vigorously. And I think they've got a very strong case. You can be sure that we're going to back them to the hilt. Now, we concede the risk that Pan Am will even favor STOL as being practical. But I think Pan Am has analyzed the situation sufficiently to realize that V/STOL is really the ultimate way to go. Whether they will state that now, with today's equipment or not, I don't know. But I think they tend to look at it that way. So we have to keep our eye on them. They could move the thing much faster than any of the other elements. One other consideration. Major reversals in airport building have taken place in the last few months: cessation of work on Miami Everglades and apparently final rejection of the Solberg site. So much time has passed, so much has been built, the civic action type of organization has gotten so far forward that there is simply not going to be a fourth airport in the New York area. It will never happen.

VI. A LOOK AHEAD

EDITOR'S INTRODUCTION

The technology that could make vast improvements in present transportation facilities already exists. Engineers and other planners have devised any number of excellent solutions to even the most complicated inner-city transit tangles. The barriers to putting these ideas into effect are financial, political, and social.

Engineers know how to improve existing subways and how to build better new ones—but where will the vast amount of money needed for such building come from? Express bus lanes would speed buses along—but would motorists stalled in adjoining lanes tolerate a special lane? The list could go on. The point is that the problems that have been outlined in this book are soluble if political and economic barriers can be breached.

In this final section we peer into the near and far future of mass transportation. The articles do not contain a consistent point of view or a consistent picture of what the future shape of transit facilities will be. Some authors predict great strides through technological innovations. Others insist that wiser use of existing facilities is the practical answer.

The first article, from *Business Week*, predicts that traffic congestion in and around the cities will get worse, not better. Predictions are for more computerization of traffic control, even electronic controls of cars entering limited access roads. Next, research engineer Sumner Myers argues that we should concentrate on existing technology to solve traffic problems. He strongly urges more attention to buses, which now account for 75 per cent of all mass transportation in the United States.

In the following articles, some of the new vehicles being tested in the United States and abroad are explained. Philip

Harrison of *Railway Age* discusses the tracked air-cushion vehicle for possible use by commuter railroads. Architect Brian Richards argues that the inner cores of cities are where the major problems lie. He outlines the features of ten new "minisystems" that are adaptable to inner-city use.

The final article takes an overview of transportation policy in cities of the future. Special emphasis, in this article from *Editorial Research Reports,* is placed on the question of whether congestion and pollution may force abandoning the gasoline auto engine in densely populated cities in favor of electric or steam cars. The real issue, the author emphasizes, is meshing the auto with other transit systems to provide maximum service for everyone.

MORE TRAFFIC JAMS TO COME [1]

Congestion—noisy, wasteful, polluting, frustrating congestion—will characterize transportation in, around, and above cities throughout the 1970s. It will become so bad that it will force New York to ban private automobiles from the middle of Manhattan Island before the conclusion of the decade.

For most of the twentieth century, Americans have taken for granted the right and ability to go anywhere at any time by any of a multitude of means. They are going to go right on believing this, building highways and buying cars and trucks and planes until, in a few key places, they run out of the one thing they cannot manufacture: space.

Actually, there are all kinds of vehicles available today—or soon to become available—that can provide more efficient transportation and keep the cities from choking. High-speed mass transit systems, such as commuter railroads, subways, or even monorails, could be built relatively easily and cheaply to relieve the congestion.

[1] Article "When Traffic Jams Stall the Nation." *Business Week.* p 186+. D. 6, '69. Reprinted from the December 6, 1969, issue of *Business Week* by special permission. Copyrighted © 1969 by McGraw-Hill, Inc.

But as Assistant Transportation Secretary Paul Chering-ton puts it: "The most efficient sleeping arrangements are those in barracks with triple-tiered bunks, and no one seri-ously suggests we should live that way." In city after city, a majority of the people has consistently failed to approve the necessary financing. In part, the voters assume that whatever is built will resemble the crowded, noisy, dirty transit systems of the Northeast. More important, no such mass transit system offers the instant door-to-door transportation pro-vided by the automobile—instant, that is, in the sense that a person can leave whenever he wants. Getting there is often less than half the fun.

Motorists' Ploy

Even in the San Francisco Bay area, a huge exception to the rule, a fascinating fact was uncovered after a $750 million bond issue just squeaked through several years ago to permit work to start on the Bay Area Rapid Transit System. A significant number of people who voted for the issue—prob-ably the difference between passage and failure—later ad-mitted they did not plan to use the high-speed trains. They voted for BART [Bay Area Rapid Transit] in the belief that enough of their neighbors would use the system to unsnarl the freeways; these voters could then have a pleasanter trip downtown in their automobiles.

Carlos C. Villarreal, Urban Mass Transportation Admin-istrator, admits BART will be in trouble at first, with pas-senger loads failing to come up to expectations right away. But it will be only a matter of time, he believes, before the scales will tip in favor of the transit system. Once commuters see that the drive into San Francisco or Oakland is too time-consuming and costly—with hardly any place downtown for parking—they will switch to BART.

In the New York metropolitan area, which already has an intricate pattern of commuter railroads, the world's largest and possibly most unpleasant subway system, and untold thousands of urban and suburban buses, the sardine-packed crowds of today will seem pleasant compared to the horrifying congestion still ahead. The millions upon millions of square feet of new office space opened up in the 1970s will require hundreds of thousands of additional workers. Call them commuters, for most of them will insist on living outside of Manhattan.

"I don't know how it's going to be done, and I don't know what streets will be involved," says Cherington. "I can't say whether it will be prohibitive tolls on the bridges and tunnels or barriers across streets or gendarmes. But this I know: There will be no private traffic in midtown Manhattan. Nothing on the drawing boards will arrive in time to save New York."

Urban Sprawl

Most U.S. cities that do not have rapid transit systems now probably will not have them. Instead, each urban area will continue to spread out until it comes up against a neighboring city growing towards it. The whole sprawl will be connected by an ever-growing grid of highways and streets to accommodate the 130 million cars and trucks expected to be registered by the early 1980s.

Yet it is impossible to build enough highways and parking lots for all these vehicles. Something will be done to ease the congestion—but only when things get so bad that a majority of the population becomes sufficiently aroused to vote for relief. And that relief may put limits on a driver's right to go where he wants.

The first steps will be tiny. A few municipalities are trying exclusive bus lanes on highways and streets. The most closely watched experiment of this type is in northern Virginia, not far from the Washington offices of the Transportation Department. One lane of a fifteen-mile stretch of Interstate 95 is set aside for express buses from the suburbs during rush hours. These buses, which are well patronized, shave fifteen to twenty minutes off the time it would take the average commuter to get to town in his own car, according to a Transportation official.

The bus lane idea will inevitably spread. Even this will take political courage to make it stick as motorist-voters sit stalled in traffic jams, glaring at empty concrete in the next lane or at an occasional, partially filled bus roaring by.

Computerization

The next step also is well within the present state of technology: using computers to control street signals and access to freeways. Again, this step will inhibit the freedom of motorists and also cost a lot. One city with computer control of traffic lights is Toronto. According to a long-time resident, the two Univacs that regulate most of the city's 870 traffic signals do a pretty good job of speeding traffic. The best measure of this, he says, is how big the traffic jams get when one of the computers breaks down.

But many U.S. cities will not vote money for the computer approach until the congestion problem gets much worse, even though there will in all probability be substantial sums of Federal money made available on a matching basis in a few years.

The really big breakthrough will come out of a combination of exclusive lanes and computer controls—with an important addition: Control equipment will have to be installed inside the vehicle. When congestion becomes intolerable in another five to ten years, this electronic solution may well be made mandatory.

In the probable chain of events, a few test highway lanes will be equipped with electronic devices to control vehicle speed. At first, only big buses will have the necessary hardware to operate in a controlled lane. The large bus has the same drawback, though to a lesser degree, as the rapid transit vehicle. It does not have enough flexibility in picking up and delivering passengers; its customers must go to it, instead of the other way around.

In time, therefore, six- to ten-passenger vehicles will circulate in bedroom communities, probably picking up passengers on call and then going to the nearest access to a controlled highway. There, they will be locked into a high-speed traffic flow, controlled from without the vehicle, that will carry them to the appropriate exit.

Eventually, private autos will be equipped to take advantage of the system. But few people think this will be widespread within the next ten years.

Freight Flow

The system also will accommodate trucks. Probably within the seventies, the forty-foot truck trailer will have to be outlawed from some downtown city streets. (If political laws do not do the job, economic laws will.) Highway tractors will pull two, three or possibly even more shorter trailers over an expanded interstate highway network. On arrival at a terminal on the outskirts of a city, the highway tractor will drop one "train" and pick up another.

The trailers will be assigned to smaller tractors equipped with the electronic control devices needed to use the controlled highway lanes. This way the flow of goods to and from widely scattered suburban and exurban shopping centers and factories will continue with the reliability required for smooth inventory control.

For the railroad industry, which could do much to alleviate congestion on the roads, the early part of the 1970s will be a turning point. Within the past few years, service and profitability have deteriorated. Many railroad presidents are of the opinion that the rate of decline is quickening.

If management, labor, and the Government do not succeed in changing conditions in a very few years, the industry will be nationalized within the next decade. "God knows, we aren't reaching out for it," said a high Government official last week. "But I'm awfully afraid it's going to be forced on us."

The problems of air traffic congestion above the biggest cities today are similar to those on the highways and streets, and so are the solutions that will evolve during the seventies.

What is planned for airplanes is, first, to get a far more accurate idea of where they are in the sky, both vertically and horizontally and then map out where each is going. Computers will plot courses that avoid collisions, and the information will move instantly, continuously, and automatically to control towers. Thus, a great many more airplanes will fit into the same amount of sky than is possible today.

Full operation of this system is at least ten years away, however. To make it work, it will be essential that all planes entering such controlled airspace come equipped with very sophisticated and very expensive electronics. The occasional flyer is not going to like it, and if he cannot afford the equipment, he will have to stay out. Even with the best electronic gear, corporate jets are going to lose some of their appeal as the skies become more crowded and delays make travel plans less reliable.

Not so long ago, many seers predicted that as communications improved—with data transmission, picture telephones, and the like—there would be less need for travel. It has not yet worked out that way. But if transportation becomes harder and more uncertain, and corrective steps are not taken, Ma Bell's "next best thing to being there" will become far better than trying to get there.

LET'S MODIFY EXISTING SYSTEMS [2]

As an engineer, I am naturally intrigued by shiny new hardware ideas. But here I want to discuss how "software"— not hardware—can bring about revolutionary improvements in urban transportation. Indeed, I feel that we must forgo technological tours-de-force and concentrate instead on how off-the-shelf technology can improve urban transportation within the next decade. That is where the action really is.... In order to provide a framework for this discussion of

[2] From "The Soft Revolution," by Sumner Myers, research engineer, Institute of Public Administration. *Architectural Forum*. 128:86-9. Ja.-F. '68. Reprinted from the Jan/Feb 1968 issue of the *Architectural Forum*. Copyright 1968 by Whitney Publications, Inc.

transportation technology, I will put forth three specific goals
—all short term and all high priority—to be implemented. . . .
Together they comprise a set of specific action-oriented goals
which are likely to be consistent with longer range and more
general transportation objectives.

Amenity, Efficiency, and Welfare

My first goal would be to improve the qualitative aspects
of urban life with higher amenity transportation. By "higher
amenity," I mean better esthetic design of stations, vehicles,
and roadways, more comfortable seats, and so on. And most
important, I include the elimination of transportation side
effects that make urban amenity impossible: noise, heat,
fumes, and especially congestion, both on the streets and in
the vehicles.

My second goal would be to increase the economic efficiency of existing systems. This is related to the first goal.
Amenity improvements will cost a good deal of money, of
course, and it is therefore especially urgent to increase the
economic efficiency of transportation systems whose amenities
are to be improved. I certainly do not mean to suggest cutting
back on service to save money. I mean instead working on
those problems which, if solved, would result in important
cost savings without degrading service.

My third goal would be to improve transportation for
those who particularly need their transportation improved—
those who cannot, for one reason or another, use an automobile. This goal requires more explanation because it runs
head on into the conventional wisdom, which holds that the
urban transportation system ought to be improved because it
benefits "everybody." The means of improvement favored
by most planners is usually some kind of rail system with
which they will rescue the city from that insolent chariot, the
automobile.

The auto lobby has infuriated the intelligentsia by arguing, in effect, that the best way to improve urban transportation for most people is to improve the auto user system. Yet

this argument cannot be dismissed out of hand. After all, four times as many city residents, on a national average, go to work by auto as by public transit, and pleasure trips are almost always by automobile. . . .

Those Without Cars

For better or worse, the design of the city, and therefore the pattern of urban life, has already been shaped by the automobile, perhaps irreversibly. With an automobile, urbanites can enjoy reasonably good access to almost all of the resources in the metropolitan area. But for people without an automobile, such access to most of the city's delights is inconvenient if not impossible.

As of 1960, over a quarter (7.3 million) of the urban households in the United States were without an automobile. Of these, 6.6 million were relatively poor households where the head of the family earned less than $6,000 per year. Twenty per cent of the nation's adult population (over seventeen years old) cannot drive—some because they don't have to or want to, but many because they are physically unable to.

While a breakdown of the data is not available, it may be assumed that a good many persons are unable to drive because of advancing age. Hopefully, poverty will be a less important constraint on auto ownership in the future, but as the number of elderly persons grows, aging will be a more important one. Even now, there are 18.5 million people over sixty-five years old.

The elderly should be encouraged to travel about the metropolitan area—to go to church, to take part in senior-center activities, to use libraries, to visit friends and relatives. If this sort of goal is to be met, public transportation must be designed to give economic door-to-door service at all times— during the off-peak hours as well as the peak hours—and to all other places in the metropolitan area as well as to its downtown.

For economic reasons rooted in old technology, public transportation systems are today primarily downtown oriented. With few exceptions, only the central business district (CBD) generates enough demand to justify the use of mass passenger vehicles—and then only for a few peak hours. Now, however, most urban travel demand is not downtown oriented. In many large cities less than 10 per cent of total person trips begin or end in the CBD. This percentage varies from a low of 7 per cent in Pittsburgh to a high of 35 per cent in Washington, D.C. Evidently, people want to go to many other places besides the CBD.

Because existing mass transportation systems do a poor job of handling this type of demand, people who are dependent on transit find themselves shut out of opportunities that other urbanites have. This is a particularly serious problem in the case of employment opportunities. . . . A recent United States Labor Department study found this to be a general problem:

Payroll employment has soared in the suburbs compared with downtown areas. . . . Many of the new jobs created by this movement could be filled by poor and unemployed city dwellers if they could get to them. [But] metropolitan transportation systems, geared to getting people to work downtown, make it even tougher for those in the city to work in the suburbs.

Transportation expert Wilfred Owen of the Brookings Institution has summed up the basic problem: "The person who for a variety of reasons has no car is increasingly barred . . . from enjoyment of what the city has to offer. Because . . . urban growth assumes the availability of private cars, everything becomes increasingly difficult to reach by other means."

While there are many people who depend on transit for their mobility, they are too few to support a transit system extensive enough to provide anything approaching the mobility that other members of the urban community have. The frequency and coverage of transit service are determined by the number of people who are willing to use transit. If these people are relatively few, the system will provide relatively little coverage and relatively infrequent service; and the mobility of those who must use such a system is correspondingly circumscribed.

If a transit system is to be extensive enough to serve its dependent users well, the system must be good enough to attract and hold a sufficient number of optional users too. This means the system must provide more than minimal service to everybody because the optional users can resort to their automobiles if they don't like the kind of service they are offered. . . .

Existing Realities

Now that a set of goals has been identified, we are ready to ask: how might technology be applied to achieve these goals? Realistically, this must be technology that can be applied to already existing transit systems. Given the depleted condition of urban pocketbooks, the multitude of other human and physical problems cities face, and the bureaucratic and legal tangles involved in city action, the forces compelling the retention of existing systems are overwhelming.

But if we cannot impose . . . [start-from-scratch] solutions in urban transportation, neither must we accept by default a widening gap between technological promise and existing realities. The existing realities are the rail systems and the bus systems, which represent the points of departure for evolutionary change. They are discussed below.

Better Rail Service

Rail transit handles demands which are relatively high and relatively predictable as to both time and origin-destination pairs (e.g., peak-hour, downtown-oriented travel). Urban railroads, particularly subways, now generally provide low amenity service and are economically inefficient.

Better rail service *might* help persuade the middle class to stay in the cities and at the same time raise the mobility and aspiration levels of the culturally deprived. It will surely improve the quality of urban life. . . . Thus, the initial objective should be to improve rail systems by relieving inhuman crowdedness, noise, dirt, and fumes, and by lowering costs to provide some of the money necessary to upgrade amenities.

The single most effective way to upgrade rail transit amenities is to reduce rush-hour crowdedness. For a given number of riders, this means either spreading the load evenly throughout the day or expanding capacity. One way to spread the peak transit load might be to stagger working hours. Another possibility is off-peak pricing.

Unfortunately, despite all the volumes written about both possibilities, nobody can say for sure that either one will work well enough to reduce the transit crush. Before spending billions on capacity expansions, one or both of these presumably cheaper alternatives should be explored. Sorely needed are some critical experiments to point the way. A critical experiment in staggering work hours would probably have to turn the city upside down. But critical experiments in off-peak pricing are entirely feasible and should be undertaken as soon as possible.

Realistically, however, we might hope for the best, but plan for the worst. If the public rejects a rational pricing system or if the experiments fail, it will be necessary to reduce crowding by expanding capacity. This means more cars at the peak and in some cases more tunnels and better signaling systems. All of this costs money—lots of it.

Some of the money required for upgrading rail transit amenities could come from reducing costs on inefficient systems. This means finding and exploiting resource-saving opportunities. At one time this would have happened as a matter of course. Forty years ago, urban rail systems were vital centers of technological innovation. Over the years, however, rail management has adopted conservative attitudes, highly skeptical of innovation. And while these attitudes are ripe for change, the process needs impetus.

A taste of success would provide some of this impetus. To assure success, the first technological projects undertaken should be low-risk ones with large and quick dollar returns.

It is relatively easy for the operations analyst to find surefire cost saving projects that will neither degrade service nor displace labor.

In short, the best way to improve existing rail systems in the near future is to apply operations research techniques to make the system more efficient. That is, the technology should begin with software, not hardware.

Moving Buses

The bus is usually given short shrift in transportation plans for the future. This is true even in the United States, where buses now carry approximately 75 per cent of all public transportation passengers. Most cities in the United States are, and will be for some time, entirely dependent on buses for mass transportation.

Even in cities with excellent subway systems, buses are practically indispensable. In New York City, over a third of the CBD workers begin the day by taking a bus to a subway station.

Buses may be important, but let's face it, they have no "tech appeal!" Cumbersome vehicles crawling through snarled city traffic seem like anachronisms in the space age. Unglamorous and inadequate as they now are, however, bus systems represent a highly promising point of departure for improving urban transportation. The reason: buses can go anywhere on rights-of-way paid for by somebody else.

This is not an insignificant factor. It means first that buses have the potential for giving door-to-door service— something that is absolutely essential if the needs of the disadvantaged are to be met. It also means that bus systems can provide chauffeured transportation at low cost.

But buses will continue to be a less than adequate means of transport as long as they get caught in traffic jams. Fortunately, this is not an insoluble problem. There are two approaches to it: put buses into lanes that are physically separate from the rest of traffic; or decongest the flow of all vehicular traffic on the streets and highways used by buses and give buses some kind of priority in the stream. The second alternative is technologically feasible and economically sensible.

In urban areas buses must for the most part continue to share their rights-of-way with other vehicles. Even separate bus lanes are wasteful of urban space except under very special conditions. As primarily journey-to-work transportation, buses would use separate lanes intensively for only twenty hours a week—and then would generally use but a fraction of the lane's vehicular capacity. A recent study in California found that separate bus lanes actually increase, rather than decrease, total person delay. The time saved by all the bus passengers would be much less than the time lost by all the auto passengers who were denied use of the relatively empty bus lane.

The approach then must be to get the whole traffic stream moving. This is really a "joint pay-off" problem: in order to decongest urban arteries for transit users, they've got to be decongested for all users, including—for better or worse —motorists.

Top Priority for Buses

Two somewhat different technologies are involved in decongesting the traffic stream. The first is flow control on limited access highways; the second is traffic control on city streets.

The first involves metering vehicles onto the highway at a rate that will hold traffic concentration below the point of greatest instability. At that point, even minor perturbations in the traffic stream cause slowdowns that may finally result in stoppages that diminish the highway's capacity. Flow control keeps highway capacity up by keeping the stream moving. Because a bus carries more people than a car, buses should be permitted to enter the flow-controlled highway "at will." Once on the highway, the bus would keep moving.

Theoretically, metered freeways should handle 6 to 8 per cent more vehicles during the peak hours. If, however, total demand were left to expand freely, as in the past, the metered freeways might attract more automobiles than the system would allow on the freeways in a given period of time. Long queues would then form on approach ramps. Presumably, this could be avoided if we had the political courage to limit aggregate demand by pricing. Of course, we do not—yet.

But even with ramp congestion, a flow control system is still highly recommended as a transit measure. Under the transit priority approach, buses would always be allowed on the highway and would therefore not be adversely affected by congestion on the ramps—thus achieving high-speed, high-volume service.

Although street traffic control is different from highway flow control, the principle of bus priority is similar. Most street traffic control systems are now programmed to move vehicles not people. All vehicles are treated equally, which means that their passengers are treated unequally. Traffic lights are set to favor three people in two cars over fifty people in one bus. In order to maximize the through-put of people, buses should be given some kind of priority in the traffic stream.

To give buses the priorities they deserve, traffic control systems must be redesigned to "count" people rather than vehicles. As matters now stand, they cannot tell a bus from a scooter or from anything else! Yet it is technically simple to sense the approach of buses in the traffic stream—by equipping them with simple transponders, for example. But the next step is experimentation, not hardware.

The Institute of Public Administration, in a consortium with Wilbur Smith Associates and Melpar Inc., has been working on some of these new operational concepts for HUD [United States Department of Housing and Urban Development]. In a recent experiment conducted for the project, traffic lights on a street in Los Angeles were manually changed to favor buses acording to how many people the buses carried. The preliminary data indicated a delay reduction of about 50 per cent for all persons in the traffic stream.

A New Flexibility

But decongesting the flow of buses answers only part of the need. What is also needed is a system that can respond dynamically to demand *as the demand occurs*—a system whose routes and schedules are not fixed in advance. When only a few people want to go to and from the same places during a short period of time, it is economically infeasible to route and schedule transit vehicles in advance to serve them well. At present, transit serves such demand poorly, if at all.

It now looks as if such a system can be developed, perhaps to give door-to-door service at costs not very much more than conventional bus service. A demand-actuated road transit (DART) system would use a vehicle like a minibus to pick up passengers (at their doors or at a bus stop) shortly after they had phoned for service. A passenger's call for service is logged in by a computer along with all other origin-destination demands currently on the system.

The computer knows the location of all its minibuses, how many passengers are on them, and where they are heading. It selects the right vehicle and dispatches it to the caller according to some optimal routing algorithm which has been programmed into the system. The system can also be designed to give the next passenger's phone a warning ring a few minutes before pickup time.

The system has a good deal of operational flexibility, and can be programmed to give different levels of service for different fares. At one extreme it might offer unscheduled single passenger door-to-door service, just like a taxi—or multipassenger service, like a jitney. At the other extreme it might offer something more like bus service, picking up passengers along a route according to a schedule specified in advance.

But even DART's bus-like service would differ from conventional bus service. The route could include several home pick-ups at extra fare. In this mode, the passenger would call only to cancel his prescheduled pickup.

The point is that DART can do what no other transit system does: it can go where the demand is and only when the demand is ready to be satisfied. The many-to-many traffic pattern to be served by DART is, of course, dominant in the low-density suburbs. But it should be emphasized that the same kind of demand can also exist in the most thickly populated sections.

Right now the automobile handles this demand for those who have access to one. For those who do not, a bus takes too long and a taxi costs too much. The cost of the taxi can be driven down by "sharing the ride," and basically the DART system is designed to accomplish this.

There is no question that a DART system will work. The question is: how well and at what cost? Preliminary data from our study indicate that, depending on demand, DART will serve its passengers not quite as fast as private taxi but at a quarter to a half of its cost.

Instant Dispatching

The hardware system that makes DART economically feasible is an automated vehicle locating (AVL) system for knowing at all times precisely where perhaps several hundred DART vehicles are. Our study shows that AVL improves the efficiency of DART's performance by 50 per cent because dispatch decisions can be made "on the fly."

The AVL system can establish the location of any vehicle with an accuracy of one hundred feet in a metropolitan area fifty miles in diameter. A central transmitter broadcasts repetitive FM command pulses continuously and at a regular rate. Each command pulse in effect addresses one particular vehicle whose equipment recognizes its own coded signal among all the others.

On receiving the coded signal, the addressed vehicle activates a keyed transmitter which produces a respond-acknowledge (R-A) signal. At least three wayside receivers pick up this R-A signal and relay it to data central. At data central, the vehicle's location is computed by triangulation using the differences in arrival times of the R-A signal at the three receivers.

The two salient features of this system are: (1) it has almost inexhaustible capacity—the system can keep track of over one million vehicles: and (2) it can be "time shared" by many different users, public and private. Thus the AVL system makes it possible to improve the urban transportation operations of police departments, trucking companies, taxi fleets and, of course, transit systems. This can be operational within five years.

The system also makes it possible to control the flow of *all* vehicles at *all* times in the metropolitan area. But this is something for the long-term future—and then only if we are willing to sacrifice personal anonymity.

TRAINS ON AIR CUSHIONS [3]

A new mode of ground transportation—the tracked air-cushion vehicle (TACV) —is coming closer to reality. In the United States, two companies are vying for a DOT [Department of Transportation] contract to build a jet-powered TACV research vehicle. Both vehicles are capable of modification for the linear induction motor (LIM) —the world's first large-scale prototype of which was unveiled last month on the West Coast. While commuter TACVs should be making the European scene within the next two years, at least one country—West Germany—is reported to be thinking of a multibillion dollar TACV freight-hauling project that could be operational by the end of the decade.

DOT's Office of High Speed Ground Transportation is interested in the TACV primarily as a new means of moving people. According to DOT statistics, about two thirds of the U.S. population lives in urban areas—this figure to rise to 80 per cent in fifteen years. . . . [The Office of High Speed Ground Transportation] sees TACV as an important stride

[3] From "TACV: Tomorrow's Mass Transport Vehicle?" by Philip Harrison, associate editor. *Railway Age.* 168:30-1. Ja. 5/12, '70. Reprinted by permission.

in high-speed transportation between cities in high-density corridors.

To this end, DOT will be closely watching the results of British and French tests, and will be getting information from the Rohr Corporation, which has bought U.S. rights to the French Aérotrain. But DOT has its own TACV research program under way and a contract for a full-size operational vehicle should be awarded sometime . . . [in 1970]. Competing for the contract are General Electric and Grumman Aerospace.

The Grumman and GE designs are for either jet or LIM propulsion. Grumman uses two jet engines to supply the air cushions. With a third jet for propulsion, the Grumman model resembles a Boeing 727 converted into a rocket sled. With the LIM, the third engine is eliminated. The Grumman TACV would be fifty-two feet long, reaching speeds between 300 and 320 mph.

General Electric's TACV design has taken a hint from spacecraft research. It is divided into command, experiment and equipment modules. The modular design permits the substitution of a LIM motor system for a 10-passenger compartment. Without LIM it utilizes four turbofan jet engines —two for propulsion and two for the air cushion. Its speed ranges between 300 and 345 mph.

LIM Who?

The linear induction motor is not as far-out as it sounds. In fact, it was first patented for rail passenger cars as far back as 1905; up until now, conventional propulsion has met all requirements. The first large-scale workable LIM was unveiled December 9, 1969, in Los Angeles when DOT and the Garrett Corporation rolled out what is claimed to be the world's first magnetically-powered research rail car.

The LIM has no moving parts, creates no air pollution, and makes little noise. Because of this, DOT has great faith in the motor as a solution to environmental problems.

In simplest terms, the LIM has two electro-magnets that are hung on opposite sides of a large central rail. An electric current is passed through the magnets. This central rail is then either attracted to the magnets or repelled. But since the rail is firmly secured to the ground and can't go anywhere, the magnets move. Since the magnets are located in the rail car, the car is pulled along for the ride.

The research LIM rail car was built for . . . [the Office of High Speed Ground Transportation] under a $3.2 million contract by the Garrett Corporation, an aerospace firm. The motor itself can provide 2,500 horsepower continuously and 5,000 horsepower for periods up to five minutes at 250 mph.

The Budd Company supplied the high-speed trucks, which are equipped with disc brakes. Halibrand Engineering built the jet-like body, Philco Ford supplied the instrumentation trailer, and Dow Chemical manufactured the thin, central reaction rail. The rail is hollow, produced in ninety-foot sections and then welded. It is twenty-one inches high, has a five-inch base and is installed down the middle of regular rail tracks.

Mating LIM to TACV could produce "a whole new breed of cat." DOT Under-Secretary James M. Beggs has gone so far as to say that it could eliminate the dependence on wheels in ground transportation.

France Is European Leader

The early advances in TACV research have come from Europe. And of all the countries involved, France is the leader.

So successful have test runs proved that French National Railways . . . is showing an interest in TACV development. The company responsible for French TACV research— Société de l'Aérotrain (SDA) —expects orders for two . . . air-cushion lines to be announced this year. These are to consist of a seventy-five-mile elevated double-track link between Paris and Orleans, and a high-speed link between Orly airport and downtown Paris. Surveyors are already preparing the Orly-Paris route, which could be ready within six months of the start of construction, according to the SDA.

If . . . [French National Railways] signs up, SDA believes other orders will follow. SDA says twenty-one countries are showing interest in French TACV work. These hopes came closer to fruition when the Rohr Corporation announced an agreement with SDA to manufacture and market the Aéro-train in the United States.

The full-scale French TACV has already chalked up speeds of 180 mph (with a 150-mph cruising speed) in test runs at Orleans. This prototype is 84 feet long and 12 feet wide, with 80 seats in a 3-2 arrangement. A half-scale model, utilizing rocket propulsion, has reached speeds of 265 mph.

The full-scale vehicle is powered by two 1,100-horsepower turbine engines which drive a reversible-pitch propeller. This mode of propulsion is to be kept for long-distance operations due to its claimed lightness and efficiency.

But the most likely power source for the projected Orly-Paris route will be the linear induction motor. SDA began testing prototype LIM's at the end of 1969.

Urba

Another French company—Compagnie d'Energétique Linéaire (CEL) —is developing an intracity TACV (the Urba) around linear induction. Two Urba eight-passenger vehicles have been tested at Lyons. They have operated both singly and coupled at speeds around thirty-nine mph. . . . [The company] maintains that speed is not of prime importance for urban transit vehicles, hence the relatively low speeds. What is important, CEL claims, is that acceleration and braking are adequate for intensive service and frequent stops.

Ultimate . . . goal is a thirty-passenger vehicle with a speed of sixty-four mph. Experiments with the full-scale vehicle are expected by the end of 1970. A 3.2-mile test track is now being completed at Lyons.

Piggyback TACVs

· Germany appears to be the first country pursuing a TACV operation as a freight mover. A task force of transport consultants and representatives of the German Federal Railway is reported to be studying a TACV for piggyback operations down the "spine" of West Germany from Hamburg to Munich—with subsequent spurs eventually linking Italy, France and the Belgian coast.

TACV trains on this line would be designed to piggyback trucks and containers at better than 250 mph. Costs of the project are estimated at a whopping $3-$5 billion. Should the project get the go-ahead, the first stretch of double-track could be operational by the end of the 1970s.

In Britain

The British government-sponsored Tracked Hovercraft Ltd. . . . is bidding for a transport contract between Heathrow airport and central London. Their research has given them confidence that they will be awarded the contract. Provided there are no problems, . . . [Tracked Hovercraft] hopes to have a TACV reach 200 mph on a four-mile test track by the end of the year. In 1971, they hope to extend the track to ten miles and gradually step up the speed.

Three test vehicles will be running by the end of the year. Two are designed to test prototype linear induction motors. The third will be a full-size version of the proposed vehicle.

MINISYSTEMS IN THE CITY [4]

Rapid transit will continue to be essential for the larger cities. It alone has the capability of bringing commuters closer to the city core or, alternatively, of encouraging the new growth of additional cores. Express buses, too, given proper road facilities, are equally useful but, like automobiles (maxi

[4] Excerpt from article by Brian Richards, a British architect and author of *New Movement in Cities. Architectural Forum.* 128:98-105. Reprinted from the Jan/Feb 1968 issue of the *Architectural Forum.* Copyright 1968 by Whitney Publications, Inc.

or mini), less able to terminate easily at any points except those peripheral to the core area. This factor may reinforce the argument to provide for good short-distance transport within cores.

It may be argued that cores will no longer be necessary in the future, and that increased phone or videophone communications will in fact enable people to stay at home. But, to date, the reverse appears to be true: people tend to congregate and move more than ever before. Automobile owners, for example, often make three times as many trips in a day as nonowners. The easier it is to move, the more people move.

But in city cores, such as those of New York or Chicago, up to 90 per cent of the people working and visiting are without their automobiles, and most short-distance trips are made on foot, by bus, or by taxi. Yet all three invariably offer deplorable service. Sidewalks are often intolerably narrow and overcrowded; bus service slow and irregular due to heavy traffic; and taxis unobtainable and expensive.

Successful experiments in which streets were closed to vehicular traffic are now well known, and some of these street closings have led to increases of trade of up to 20 per cent. Experiments with minibuses running at close intervals have been successful, as in Washington, D.C., and have proved conclusively the need, on some streets, for such systems. Only with taxis, the most flexible of all systems, have experiments lagged behind. The jitney, or shared taxi, was common in the United States in the thirties and is operating successfully in many foreign cities.

All three systems—walking, bus, and taxi—offer the easiest and most economical way of getting around in cities. Rapid transit in the city core is often, for reason of size, placed underground at a high cost. (Capital costs per two-track mile of cut-and-cover construction may be assumed to be $17.5 million.) Partly for this reason, only a limited network has been provided in the city core, making its use for short-distance trips far from ideal. Also, compared with surface-level or elevated transport, it disorients the passenger within the city—an important factor where, on shopping or visiting trips, experience and enjoyment of the scene are essential.

On the streets of the city, traffic termed "essential," such as service trucks and vans, clog movement and result in poor travel times for taxis and buses. And traffic-engineering measures to improve flow (e.g., one-way streets) increasingly negate the convenience of buses. In Washington, D.C., for example, although the minibus runs at $2\frac{1}{2}$-minute intervals, average journey speed is only $4\frac{1}{2}$ mph; average trip length is six city blocks; and eleven buses are required for a circuit of $1\frac{1}{2}$ miles. And so, because of the dense traffic in our cities, the subway, for those cities possessing one, may still be quicker to take for short trips of one half mile because it is segregated from other traffic—although it was not designed for short trips.

Elevated rapid transit has been proposed for several cities, ranging from the Monorail at Seattle to the recently rejected guided bus system proposed for Manchester, England. But few city streets are wide enough to take the large scale structures required—and again, as with the underground, they are not designed to solve problems of short-distance movement.

Small-Scale Systems

Research and development are now under way in the United States and in Great Britain with systems small enough in scale to be acceptable when running above the city street. Some of these are slow enough to permit station spacing at close intervals (one quarter mile), and many are likely to prove cheap enough both to construct and operate so that fine-mesh networks would be profitable. It is undoubtedly this kind of transport facility for which there now exists a latent demand in many of our cities.

The basic requirements of such a small-scale system are these: (1) it must be capable of integration into the "inherited environment"; (2) it must be available for operation eighteen hours a day; (3) it should involve no waiting and must be easily accessible; (4) it should operate on low fares, or possibly be free of charge; (5) it should be silent, free from fumes, and safe; (6) it should be open-ended, capable of change, addition, or easy removal; (7) it should have a variable capacity and ability to handle certain goods and deliveries; (8) it should have an average speed of fifteen mph —twice the current average in many cities; and (9) it should be enjoyable to ride on.

No system of secondary movement having all the above requirements is manufactured today, although several are under study by firms in the United States and elsewhere. Many systems, such as multispeed moving pavements, have been tried with success at expositions over the past seventy years, but no single transport authority has been prepared to consider their validity in the context of city-center transport. Three factors, however, may lead to introduction of short-distance movement technology: the rising cost of manpower (bus drivers' wages often represent 60 per cent of operating costs); public demand for better public transport; and the increase in traffic congestion.

The systems discussed on the . . . [following] pages are all small in scale and therefore capable of running above street level or even through buildings. They are likely to have high initial capital costs but low operating costs when fully automated systems are available. Maintenance costs are likely to be high, but this will depend on the complexity of the technology. No mention is made here of this factor, which is, of course, an extremely critical one.

Carveyor

Designed by Stephens-Adamson and Goodyear, the Carveyor was studied first in 1954 as a system to run underground and replace the [New York] Times Square–Grand Central shuttle. An actual full-scale prototype was tested successfully. As the operating staff would have been minimal, it is understood that union difficulties effectively blocked its installation.

In this system, cabins with from four to ten seats run on a track at fifteen mph, with boarding platforms at 400-yard intervals. The latter consists of pedestrian conveyors, parallel to the track, and moving at the same speed as the cabins (1½ mph), for people to board or leave in safety. The capacity of the system ranges from 5,000 to 11,000 seated passengers per hour in one direction, depending on cabin size.

In the rapid transit plan for Los Angeles, prepared by Daniel, Mann, Johnson & Mendenhall, the Carveyor was one of the systems considered for downtown distribution. Atlanta proposes to use it in its rapid transit plan, also as a distribution system. Victor Gruen, in his plan for New York's Welfare Island, proposed using the Carveyor to run the two-mile length of the island as the principal system of internal transportation.

Only one known comparable system, the Carlator, is operating today—in a recreation park in Japan. . . . After running three years, it has achieved an annual capacity of over a million people, at a maximum rate of 3,000 passengers an hour.

Cost estimates of the Carveyor vary from $4.8 million to $7.4 million per mile for a two-way installation, and Federal funds are now being sought for a half-mile demonstration line.

Dashaveyor

This system is relatively unknown as yet in the transport field, but is considered by mechanical handling specialists to be one of the most technically advanced and robust systems developed to date. Designed by the Dashaveyor Company, it consists of small six-seater cabins, called "modules" . . . which run within an enclosed tubular guideway. The modules can operate singly or in "flights" of up to twenty cars. . . . The modules are electrically propelled and remote-controlled to slow down, empty, fill up, and accelerate to speeds of up to eighty mph. The system is capable of running horizontally, vertically, up and down inclines—even under water.

A five-mile installation has operated for over a year at a copper mine in Michigan, and the system is considered ready for application to the field of public transport. A number of public agencies already have expressed interest in the new system, the company claims.

Peoplemover

Designed by WED Enterprises and Goodyear, the People-mover is an automatic, continuously moving system. It consists of four-seater cabins running at seven mph on an elevated guideway six feet wide; and it has a capacity of 4,800 people an hour. Stations consist of revolving circular platforms, around which the cabins circle at the same speed, doors opening automatically.

The Peoplemover is being developed as a transport system for use in Disney's new Florida city of EPCOT [Experimental Prototype Community of Tomorrow], where the tracks will radiate from the central shopping and business zone out into the residential areas, reducing the need for parking in the center. The system has been operating successfully at Disneyland since September [1967]. . . . Although the circular boarding platforms likely would be too large for use in dense city centers, parallel conveyor belts would consume less space.

Minirail

Designed by Habegger of Switzerland, the Minirail consists of a series of small twelve-seat cabins joined into trains. It runs on a twin steel-channel track under automatic driverless control at speeds of up to fifteen mph.

The system operated at Montreal's Expo 67, carrying 5,400 people per hour over an elevated track through the grounds. Its function was primarily that of a sightseeing system, generally with a one-way track and relatively few stations. Unfortunately, due to high demand, the system became overloaded.

(At Lausanne, incidentally, the Minirail ran over, under, and straight through several of the buildings . . . demonstrating its adaptability to difficult urban situations.)

The Montreal system and the two previous installations at Munich . . . and Lausanne used open-air cabins designed specifically for exhibition use. More recent designs use cabins that are fully enclosed and have automatic doors. The most recent serious proposal by an authority for its use is at Haringay, North London, where it is intended as a connector system between car parks, the main shopping center, and the underground station.

Installation and operating costs are low: the Lausanne system, with a 20-cent fare, paid for all development and operating costs after running six months.

Guide-o-matic Train

Designed by Barrett Electronic Corporation, this system uses a small-scale train that follows a guidance cable laid in the floor. It is now being installed as an underground circulation system at Houston Airport. . . .

Each train . . . consists of three eight-seater coaches and a forward "power unit" containing batteries that supply power to dual rear-wheel motors. Built of aluminum and fiber glass, each train is 7 feet 6 inches high, 5 feet wide, and 45 feet long.

A four-train system, such as that at Houston Airport, can handle two hundred passengers in a ten-minute peak period, with a maximum hourly capacity of about 1,200 people. Operation is fully automatic, requiring no driver. An electronic monitor on each train sends malfunction alerts to a central control station, where an attendant mans an electronic console.

Transit Expressway

Developed by Westinghouse Electric Corporation, the Transit Expressway, or Skybus, is larger in scale than the other systems discussed here. It is intended primarily as a commuter system for medium-density areas. In 1965, a 9,340-

foot test loop was installed in Pittsburgh's South Park . . . where some 135,000 passengers rode the system in two years. The Port Authority of Allegheny County now plans to build an operating Skybus shuttle line between the Golden Triangle and a suburban area.

The electrically propelled Skybus cars run on four pairs of pneumatic tires along an elevated steel roadway topped with concrete "tracks" twenty-two inches wide. The cars are stabilized and locked in place by sets of chassis-mounted horizontal guide wheels which engage a steel "guide beam" between the tracks.

The Skybuses would operate twenty-four hours a day, using single vehicles during off-peak hours, and linking them into trains of up to ten cars at peak times. The maximum speed is fifty mph, and load-carrying capacity is 21,000 passengers per hour.

The trains are fully automatic, requiring no motorman, conductor, or attendant on board. They are so quiet, claims Westinghouse, that they could operate inside a building without disturbing its occupants.

For large cities, Westinghouse foresees the use of the Skybus as an outlying feeder for the central rail rapid-transit system. In smaller urban areas, where it would be the central system, its outer parts would be served by feeder buses.

Teletrans

This system, now under study by the Teletrans Corporation, consists of four-seat cars running on an elevated track under computer control. . . . Passengers at each station . . . receive a card punched with their intended destination, which they take to the first car waiting in line. After the card has been inserted into a slot, car doors close and the car accelerates automatically to merge with others passing on the main track. The car runs directly, with no intermediate stops, to the required station, where it is switched into a siding, ready for the next passenger. Teletrans are now under contract from American Airlines for a study of the system at small scale applied to baggage handling in airports. In Great Britain, a government contract was recently awarded to the Brush Electrical Engineering Company to develop a system having similar operating characteristics. A full-scale prototype will be tested.

Both systems claim theoretical capacities of 20,000 people per hour, which could make them suitable for metropolitan use. But the feasibility of Teletrans within existing cities will partly depend on the method of handling cars at stations. A need for large sidings at stations could mean that only extensive and costly land purchase would make the system usable above ground in dense urban areas.

Transveyor

Designed by the Battelle Institute of Geneva, in cooperation with Sud-Aviation, the Transveyor is now under development for use in the new Paris Nord Airport and should be operational within two years. It consists of a series of platforms about 6 feet square onto which the passenger steps, as onto an escalator. Doors close first in front, then behind. The platform then accelerates to fifteen mph, until slowing down at the end of the trip, when the reverse procedure occurs. . . .

At present the design is intended for use between points with no intermediate stops. It is suitable for use in a situation such as a shopping center parking lot, where a distance of half a mile or more is too long for a normal pedestrian conveyor. Capacities are estimated at seven thousand people an hour, and the system is small enough to run elevated. Boarding platforms require about twelve feet of depth, sufficient for the system to turn around.

Overground in London

British architect Brian Richards, author of the preceding . . . [sections of this article] on promising new movement systems for dense urban areas, is himself engaged in a study to apply a small elevated system to the Central Area of London. Richards and transportation economist J. M. Thomson are proposing a system employing four- or eight-passenger cars which travel within a plexiglass-enclosed tube twelve feet in diameter. They would run twenty feet above the center of major wide streets in the area . . . with escalators and stairs leading down to sidewalks at the station. . . .

The system would connect with an inner ring of parking garages around the Central Area, and with the stations of the subway system. It would also handle the movement of light goods with service capsules placed on the line at special points. Richards and Thomson envision the eventual integration of the system into new air-rights developments of buildings and pedestrian ways.

The cars would travel at fifteen mph, seventy-five feet apart, and bunch together at stations, where they would slow to the same speed as two fifty-foot-long parallel pedestrian conveyors. Doors would open for thirty seconds to permit boarding or leaving the cars. Capacity is 6,000 people per hour in each direction.

Swoosh!

In the eyes of a number of transportation experts, the most promising device currently being proposed for future high-speed transport within and between urban areas is Gravity-Vacuum Transit (GVT), a system developed by aeronautical engineer Lawrence K. Edwards, president of Tube Transit Corporation in Palo Alto, California.

As its name implies, GVT employs gravity and vacuum to propel trains—at enormous speeds—through a pair of steel tubes imbedded in underground tunnels. . . . The basic steps of the system's automatic operation [are]:

1. While the train is resting in station A, surrounded by normal atmosphere, air in the tube section between it and station B is evacuated.

2. Valve A is opened, and the train is pushed into the tube incline by atmospheric pressure aided by gravity.

3. As the train approaches station B, valve A is closed; air behind the train is expanded while air ahead is compressing.

4. Valve B opens when air in the tube returns to atmospheric pressure, and the train's momentum carries it into station B.

5. The train stops in station B, again surrounded by normal atmosphere—and the five-step process begins again.

For stability, the trains would travel on rails, but no on-board engines would be required for propulsion. Lawrence claims that GVT is capable of speeds roughly twice the limit for any other system, existing or proposed. He also says that GVT would be much cheaper to build and operate.

The Regional Plan Association of New York, which considers GVT's potential "almost too good to be true," has proposed that it be incorporated in future transit plans for the region—subject to its being tested out with a full-scale demonstration model. For that purpose, Lawrence needs an estimated $10 million, which is about a fifth of the cost of a single moon-landing vehicle.

TRANSPORTATION POLICY IN CITIES OF THE FUTURE [5]

Whatever its merits as a source of automotive power, the gasoline engine is choking urban civilization with its fumes. Whether the engine can be muzzled or must be scrapped is at the heart of a public policy debate taking shape in Washington and Detroit. Perhaps the gasoline engine can survive without impairing the health of mankind if it is used in combination with other power sources. The Cornell Aeronautical Laboratory of Buffalo, New York, in a study made for the Commerce Department in 1965, suggested the desirability of two distinct types of vehicles, one for urban

[5] From "Steam and Electric Autos," by Gertrude S. Rubin, staff writer. *Editorial Research Reports.* 2 no 6:597-601. Ag. 14, '68. Reprinted by permission.

use only and the other solely for highway travel. The Cornell group predicted that a major market for electric automobiles, primarily for urban use, would appear by 1980.

Howard K. Smith, writing in the June 1966 issue of *The Washingtonian,* asserted that dozens of things could be done about city traffic "when the moment of total paralysis and the incidence of lung and throat ailments finally prove that something must be done." One idea is to rent drive-it-your-self electric carts to downtown motorists. Smith said there were few inner cities that could be traversed faster today in a Cadillac than half a century ago in a horse-drawn buggy.

The commuter car market alone is promising for electric vehicles. Commerce Department statistics show that 60 per cent of passenger vehicle trips taken by the motoring public are of less than five miles, and 95 per cent are of less than thirty miles. Short trips account for more than 58 per cent of the total mileage driven by American motorists. With these figures in mind, the Federal Power Commission projected sales of 1.5 million to 2 million electric passenger cars by 1980 and 3 million to 4 million by 1985.

Such projections assume that an electric will become the family's second, or third, car. If it is confined to this status, a number of experts contend, neither production nor pollution problems will be solved. But there appears to be hope in automotive engineering circles that a hybrid car can be perfected—powered by batteries in urban areas and by another power source, gasoline or steam or something more exotic, in the open country.

Richard S. Morse of MIT contends that steam is ideally suited to city bus operations because of low noise and pollution factors. At the request of the Department of Housing and Urban Development, a study was made recently by Energy Systems, Inc., to determine the likelihood of replacing diesel engines currently used in buses of large cities with steam power. Technical findings to date indicate that the steam engine compares favorably with the diesel in buses. These findings give rise to suggestions that a combination of steam engines for big vehicles and electric for small ones will ultimately serve the cities best.

To accelerate solution of the pollution problem created by automobiles, Lloyd D. Orr, professor of economics at Indiana University, would have the Federal Government give financial support to a wide range of promising propulsion systems.

The most satisfactory solution to automobile air pollution problems [Orr testified at the Senate hearing on steam-propelled cars, May 27, 1968] ultimately lies in the design of vehicles which are attractive to the consumer and inherently free of toxic emissions. A public policy which encourages the development of such vehicles is in the long run much more compatible with the private enterprise system than an entire phalanx of Federal and state regulations designed to reduce the level of emissions from the I-C [internal combustion] engine to acceptable levels.

The Federal Government could promote changes in Detroit by making outright grants to encourage innovation and by setting new standards for motor vehicles it purchases. Washington used its purchasing power to prod auto manufacturers to install new safety devices before Federal law required them. In January 1965 the General Services Administration, purchasing agent for the Federal Government, issued a list of seventeen safety features it would require on all motor vehicles ordered after April 1966. The retooling required to add those features on 36,000 nonmilitary vehicles sold to the Government in the fiscal year 1967 resulted in weakening Detroit's resistance to installing them on the same models for general sales. In the same way, the Federal Government might conceivably set its standards in a way to promote innovations in automotive propulsion.

Senator [Warren G.] Magnuson [Democrat, Washington] introduced bills in 1967 to authorize appropriation of . . . funds for automobile pollution research. One . . . would have authorized the Department of Transportation to spend $10.5 million over a three-year period to develop fuel-cell or battery systems for electric automobiles and to "design, construct and test" prototype vehicles. The other bill would have authorized the Department of Health, Education, and Welfare to spend $5 million on research into low-pollution methods of propelling vehicles. The Administration opposed both bills. [Former] Secretary of Transportation Alan S. Boyd told the Senate Commerce Committee in March 1967 that "research on electric vehicles is first and foremost a responsibility of private industry." He said the job of the Federal Government was to set performance standards and encourage industry to take action.

Competition of Automobiles With Mass Transit

Public policy has to take into account how new propulsion for automobiles would fit into the total transportation system of the future—a system embracing both mass transit and single vehicles. Urban critics say the automobile too often competes with, rather than complements, mass transit. For example, the average daily number of cars entering New York City rose from 382,000 in 1948 to 590,000 in 1960, but the average number of people entering the city declined in the same period from 3.7 million to 3.3 million. Commuter railroads serving the nation's major cities are in various stages of disrepair and bankruptcy, while the lanes of motor traffic in and out of the cities become more jammed year by year.

Today more than 70 per cent of the country's 200 million people live in urban areas, up from 64 per cent in 1950. Nine of every ten of today's urban dwellers are found in what the United States Census Bureau defines as the nation's 224 metropolitan areas. The National Planning Association predicts that by 1975 some 164 million people, or 73 per cent of the population total expected by that time, will live in metropolitan areas—with 60 per cent of the total population concentrated in the twenty-five largest areas.

Some urbanologists think the time is coming when the combination of air pollution and traffic congestion will force older cities like Boston, New York and Philadelphia to restrict use of private automobiles. The Department of Housing and Urban Development has awarded four contracts for the study of ways to improve urban transportation in the foreseeable future. These study contracts, though small, may help to identify programs that would promote a more unified transportation system. However, the next decade or so is expected to be a time of evaluation rather than development. Max L. Feldman, author of a transportation study for General Electric, has said: "It can be hoped that changes and improvements will be evident by 1980. . . . By the year 2000 there should be some significant changes in urban transportation."

Feldman thinks that the automobile as now known will be around for a long time. No other vehicle to equal its convenience and flexibility has yet been found. Great social change must occur before the automobile can be dislodged from its present dominant position in the American transportation system. Yet air pollution and city congestion may well force the pace of social change. Whether the automobile can withstand the generally rising pressure for change will depend on the ability of modern technology to remold the vehicle in a way that is less harmful to its environment.

There is long-range hope that some new schemes in corporate "think tanks" and on the drawing board will allow urban Americans to retain their cherished cars without polluting and cluttering the landscape. Fifty or more proposals have been advanced in recent years to make the automobile an integral component of a mass transit system. Most of the proposals look toward operation of individual electric cars on roadways where power would be fed to them as they moved along, and where their speed, entry and exit would be controlled by the system. Such an approach was proposed by General Electric around 1960. It was followed by a demonstration StaRRcar developed b ythe Alden Self-Transit Systems Corporation. The traveler in the age of StaRRcar leaves home in a rented vehicle and drives a short distance on regular roads under power from electric batteries. He then switches onto a specially designed guideway, dials his destination, and is automatically switched off upon reaching it. For his trip home, he obtains another StaRRcar at a rental station in the city.

Another proposal seemingly from the pages of science fiction is the Stephens-Adamson-Goodyear Carveyor system. It is conceived as a downtown distribution system which would place passengers in specially designed vehicles carried from one part of town to another on a conveyor belt. Still another new system is the Disney WEDway [See "Mini-systems in the City" in this section, above.—Ed.]. A WEDway has been installed in the new Tomorrowland at Disneyland in Anaheim, California. Propelled by wheels powered in the system's roadway, four-passenger vehicles climb steep grades, negotiate sharp curves, and even ascend a helix.

Since we have both the technology and the desire for better transportation [a professor at Massachusetts Institute of Technology has written], it seems that all the elements necessary for a real breakthrough in transportation are present. In actuality, however, there is hardly a more difficult transition than that between the conceptual development of an innovation in transportation and its implementation. The difficulty is accentuated by the magnitude of the undertaking as well as by the division of financial responsibility between the public and private sectors of the economy. At the root of the difficulties lies the problem of securing adequate financing to implement innovations in transportation.

Whether today's far-out systems will become tomorrow's common modes of travel, no one knows. But bold ideas are now commanding a respectful hearing among transportation planners. In the meantime, long-suffering urban commuters await more modest and more quickly attainable relief.

BIBLIOGRAPHY

An asterisk (*) preceding a reference indicates that the article or a part of it has been reprinted in this book.

BOOKS, PAMPHLETS, AND DOCUMENTS

Adams, C. F. Railroads: their origin and problems. Harper. '69.

American Transit Association. Transit fact book, 1969. American Transit Association. 815 Connecticut Ave. NW. Washington, D.C. 20006.

Berghaus, Erwin. The history of the railways. Barrie & Rockliff. '64.

Berry, D. S. The technology of urban transportation. Northwestern University Press. '62.

Body, Geoffrey, ed. Railway enthusiasts' handbook 1969-70. Kelley.

Burch, P. H. Highway revenue and expenditure policy in the United States. Rutgers University Press. '62.

Cherington, C. R. Regulation of railroad abandonments. Harvard University Press. '48.

Cohen, L. B. Work staggering for traffic relief: an analysis of Manhattan's central business district. Praeger. '68.

Committee for Economic Development. Developing metropolitan transportation policies. The Committee. 477 Madison Ave. New York 10022. '65.

Danielson, M. N. Federal-metropolitan politics and the commuter crisis. Columbia University Press. '65.

Davis, J. L. Elevated system and the growth of northern Chicago. Northwestern University Press. '65.

Dickey, J. W. Mass transit. (Exch. bibl. 98-99). Council of planning librarians. Box 229. Monticello, Ill. 61856. '69.

Dodge, R. V. Rails of the Silver Gate. Golden West.

Donovan, F. R. Wheels for a nation. Crowell. '65.

Duke, Donald, ed. City and interurban cars. Golden West. '66.

Friedlaender, A. F. Interstate highway system: a study in public investment. Humanities Press. '65.

Griswold, W. E. The urban transportation dilemma, an operational solution. The Author. Cambridge, Mass. '70.
    Report to be published in Papers of the 11th Annual Meeting of the Transportation Research Forum. R. B. Cross. Oxford, Ind.

Haefele, E. T. ed. Transport and national goals. Brookings Institution. '69.

Hibbs, John. Transport for passengers. (Institute of Economic Affairs. Hobart Paper, No. 23). Transatlantic. '63.

Hilton, G. W. and Due, J. F. Electric interurban railways in America. Stanford University Press. '60.

Horton, Frank, ed. Geographic studies of urban transportation and network analysis. Northwestern University Press. '68.

Keats, John. The insolent chariots. Lippincott. '60.

Kirkland, E. C. Men, cities and transportation; a study in New England history 1820-1900. Russell & Russell. '68.

Klose, Dietrich. Metropolitan parking structures. Praeger. '65.

Lang, A. S. and Soberman, R. M. Urban rail transit. Massachusetts Institute of Technology [for the Joint Center for Urban Studies of MIT and Harvard Univ.]. '64.

Lansing, J. B. Transportation and economic policy. Free Press. '66.

Lansing, J. B. and Hendricks, Gary. Automobile ownership and residential density. University of Michigan, Institute for Social Research. Ann Arbor, Mich. 48105. '67.

Leinwand, Gerald, ed. Traffic jam. Washington Square Press. '69.

Locklin, D. P. Economics of transportation. Irwin. '66.

Martin, B. V. and others. Principles and techniques of predicting future demand for urban area transportation. MIT Press. '65.

Massachusetts Institute of Technology. The glideway system. The Institute. '66.

Massachusetts Institute of Technology. Project Metran: an integrated, evolutionary transportation system for urban areas; Mark E. Hanson, ed. The Institute. '66.

Meyer, J. R. The urban transportation problem. Harvard University Press. '65.

Meyer, J. R. and others. Economics of competition in the transportation industries. Harvard University Press. '59.

Miller, J. A. Fares, please. D. Appleton-Century. '41; P. Smith.

National Committee on Urban Transportation. Better transportation for your city. Public Administration Service. 1313 E. 60th St. Chicago 60637. '58.

Nelson, J. C. Railroad transportation and public policy. Brookings Institution. '59.

Oi, W. Y. and Shuldiner, P. W. An analysis of urban travel demands. Northwestern University, Transportation Center. 1810 Hinman Ave. Evanston, Ill. 60201. '62.

Ornati, O. A. and others. Transportation needs of the poor; a case study of New York City. Praeger. '69.

Owen, Wilfred. Cities in the motor age. Viking. '59.
Owen, Wilfred. The metropolitan transportation problem. Brookings Institution. '66.
Owen, Wilfred. Strategy for mobility. Brookings Institution. '64.
Palmer, Phil, and Palmer, Mike. Cable cars of San Francisco. Howell-North. '59.
Pell, Claiborne. Megalopolis unbound. Praeger. '66.
Richards, Brian. New movement in cities. Reinhold. '66.
Riegel, R. E. The story of the western railroads: from 1852 through the reign of the giants. University of Nebraska Press. '64.
Roth, G. J. Parking space for cars. Cambridge University Press. '66.
Roth, G. J. Paying for parking. Institute of Economic Affairs. Eaton House, Eaton Square, London, S.W. 1, England.
Sampson, R. J. and Farris, M. T. Domestic transportation; practice, theory and policy. Houghton. '66.
Schneider, L. M. Marketing urban mass transit. Harvard University, Graduate School of Business Administration, Division of Research. Soldiers Field. Boston, Mass. 02163. '65.
Sharp, Clifford. Problems of urban passenger transport. Leicester University Press. '67.
Smerk, G. M. Urban transportation: the Federal role. Indiana University Press. '65.
Snow, W. B. ed. The highway and the landscape. Rutgers University Press. '59.
Thomas, D. StJ. The rural transport problem. Routledge. '63.
Transportation Center Library. A reference guide to metropolitan transportation; an annotated bibliography. The Library. Northwestern University. Evanston, Ill. 60201. '64.
Wilson, G. W. and others. Impact of highway investment on development. Brookings Institution. '66.
Wingo, Lowdon, Jr. Transportation and urban land. Johns Hopkins Press. '61.

PERIODICALS

American City. 83:92-3. N. '68. How to make mass transit work in the smaller city. T. G. Steinbach.
American City. 84:59-62. N. '69. Urban transportation tomorrow. J. A. Volpe.
American City. 84:8. D. '69. Mass transportation, what works and why.
*Architectural Forum. 128:47-114. Ja.-F. '68. Traffic in cities; symposium.
    Reprinted in this book: The soft revolution. Sumner Myers. p86-9; Minisystems in the city. Brian Richards. p98-105.

Architectural Record. 145:9. My. '69. Are highways seven times
    more important than cities? W. F. Wagner, Jr.
Audubon. 71:4-11. Jl. '69. Superjetport, or Everglades Park? Paul
    Brooks.
Aviation Week. 89:16-17. Jl. 22, '68. Congestion crisis jams air-
    ways. K. J. Stein.
Aviation Week. 91:24. D. 15, '69. Rail vehicle completed for test
    of linear induction propulsion.
Aviation Week. 92:39-41+. My. 18, '70. Eastern studies air-shuttle
    improvements. J. P. Woolsey.
Aviation Week. 92:41+. My. 25, '70. Local service airline support
    scrutinized. H. D. Watkins.
*Bergen County Record. p 1+. S. 12, '67. Railroad decline com-
    pounds area's transportation woes. E. J. Flynn.
*Bergen County Record. p 1+. S. 13, '67. Commuter buses run at
    a deficit. E. J. Flynn.
Business Week. p 180+. O. 21, '67. More zip for the fastest train;
    Japan's new Tokaido line.
Business Week. p 64-6+. Mr. 9, '68. Saving New York from
    strangling.
Business Week. p 128+. Jl. 13, '68. Is the passenger train riding
    into history?
Business Week. p 25. Ag. 3, '68. Highways get a lift; Federal-Aid
    Highway Act of 1968.
Business Week. p 111-12. D. 14, '68. Giving people a voice on
    highways; public hearing requirements on Federal-Aid high-
    way projects.
Business Week. p 76-7. Ag. 30, '69. Jets vs. the call of the wild.
Business Week. p 74-5. O. 18, '69. Will success spoil the Metroliner?
Business Week. p 144+. O. 18, '69. Biggest snarl on city highways;
    Baltimore freeway program.
Business Week. p 94-6+. N. 15, '69. What delayed the jumbo jets.
Business Week. p 100+. N. 15, '69. New fares for new planes?
Business Week. p 158. N. 22, '69. Piggybackers all fall down but
    railroads look for a pickup.
Business Week. p 76-7+. N. 29, '69. Looking for a traffic cop in
    the sky; anti-collision devices.
*Business Week. p 186+. D. 6, '69. When traffic jams stall the na-
    tion; forecast for the 1970s.
Business Week. p54-6. D. 20, '69. New Haven RR: the road to ruin.
Business Week. p 56-7. Ja. 3, '70. Where commuting by train is
    a pleasure.
Business Week. p 109-10. Ja. 17, '70. When a railroad makes the
    rules.

Business Week. p 78-9. Ja. 31, '70. How the 747 came to fly; inaugural flight.

*Business Week. p 60-71. Mr. 14, '70. The story behind the commuter crisis.

Business Week. p 68. Mr. 28, '70. A derailment at last chance junction?

Business Week. p 58-9. Je. 6, '70. The SST: sitting duck for budget cutters.

Business Week. p 92+. Je. 20, '70. The Penn Central's troubles branch out.

Business Week. p 56. Jl. 11, '70. Tokyo monorail wins its comeback fight.

Christian Science Monitor. p 9. Ap. 27, '65. Speeding the traffic. A. D. Hughes.

*Christian Science Monitor. p 18. S. 25, '69. Tolls urged to ease the traffic jams. R. W. McManus.

*Christian Science Monitor. p 5. Mr. 25, '70. Pity the poor commuter. R. W. McManus.

Columbia Journal of World Business. 2:47-53. N./D. '67. Wanted: the air-truck-rail-water-bus company. W. H. Tucker.
    Based on address before the School of Journalism, Columbia University, May 8, 1967.

*Congressional Digest. 48:289-314. D. '69. Controversy over Federal methods of financing aid to urban transit systems: pro and con.

Dun's Review. 93:30-3+. F. '69. Mass transit, and frustrated executives. M. F. Brdlik.

Editorial Research Reports. 1 no 8:143-60. F. 22, '67. Airport modernization. Jeanne Kuebler.

*Editorial Research Reports. 2 no 6:585-601. Ag. 14, '68. Steam and electric autos. G. S. Rubin.

Editorial Research Reports. 2 no 10:671-88. S. 10, '69. Jumbo jets: new travel era. H. B. Shaffer.

Environment. 12:22-7. My. '70. Onward and upward; technical, environmental, and economic problems of supersonic air transportation. K. H. Hohenemser.

Esquire. 71:62-7. F. '69. Electric solution to the traffic problem: MIT's guideway system.

Flying. 82:52-60+. F. '68. Air traffic.

Forbes. 104:182-4. Ja. 1, '70. Transportation: department of its own.

Forbes. 105:23-4. Ap. 15, '70. Superjet!

Forbes. 105:62-3. Je. 1, '70. Here come the buses.

Forbes. 105:23-4. Je. 15, '70. Detroit: a new era.

Fortune. 75:177+. Ap. '67. Subways don't have to be miserable.

Fortune. 77:116-19+. Mr. '68. Airlines' turbulent new economics. C. J. V. Murphy.

Fortune. 78:158-63+. N. '68. Wheels-up time for STOL. Tom Alexander.

*Fortune. 81:105-10. D. '69. Mexico's subway is for viewing. A. F. W. Liversidge.

Fortune. 82:104-9+. Ag. '70. The Penn Central bankruptcy express. Rush Loving, Jr.

Holiday. 46:60-1+. D. '69. Master train of France: the Mistral. J. R. Roberson.

Life. 62:39-43. My. 12, '67. Bitterest fight: new mass transit vs. more highways. Chris Welles.

Life. 65:38-47. Ag. 9, '68. Crisis of the cluttered air; with report by John Saar.

Life. 65:26B. Ag. 23, '68. Highway bill we could live without.

Life. 66:24D-35. My. 30, '69. Highway as a killer.

Living Wilderness. 33:13-20. Spring '69. Jetport and the Everglades; life or runaway?

Mechanics Illustrated. 66:44-5. Ja. '70. Travel in the '70s. K. E. Ludvigsen.

Monthly Labor Review. 91:37-9. Ag. '68. Federal highway programs and employment. J. I. Walsh.

Motor Trend. 21:48-51. Ap. '69. In defense of the automobile. L. Levine.

Nation. 207:529-32. N. 18, '68. Pork in big barrels; excerpt from Highways or people. A. Q. Mowbray.

Nation. 210:207-11. F. 23, '70. Steam car may save us. A. Q. Mowbray.

National Geographic. 133:194-219. F. '68. Our growing Interstate Highway System. R. P. Jordan.

National Geographic. 136:301-41. S. '69. Coming revolution in transportation. F. C. Appel.

Nation's Business. 57:84-6. O. '69. Congress at the crossroads; decisions on aid expansion.

*New Republic. 156:11-12. My. 27, '67. The jetport tangle. Walter Pitkin, Jr.

*New York Times. p 20. Mr. 3, '66. Text of the message on transportation sent to Congress by President Johnson.

New York Times. p E 7. D. 31, '67. "White roads through black bedrooms." B. D. Ayres, Jr.

New York Times. p 44. Ja. 28, '68. Freeway planning struggle in Washington may determine shape of nation's urban highway system.

New York Times. p 37+. D. 10, '69. Ground is broken for subway-surface line in capital. B. A. Franklin.

New York Times. p 40. D. 26, '69. Irate citizens across the nation are vigorously resisting the construction of jetports. Robert Lindsey.

New York Times. p 44. Ja. 16, '70. Mechanical bugs still plague Metroliners after year in service. Robert Lindsey.

New York Times. p 22. F. 3, '70. Highway construction remains mainstay in transport outlay. Christopher Lydon.

*New York Times. p 39+. F. 16, '70. Easy ride on a Philadelphia transit line. Robert Lindsey.

New York Times. p 28. Mr. 11, '70. Of nation's storied passenger trains, little is left but names and memories. Christopher Lydon.

New York Times. p 86. My. 10, '70. FAA begins reforms air controllers want. Robert Lindsey.

New York Times. p E 3-4. My. 31, '70. SST: arguments louder than sonic boom. Christopher Lydon.

New York Times. p 70. Je. 1, '70. Boeing 747: the first 120 days of the jumbo's reign. Robert Lindsey.

New York Times. p 30. Jl. 28, '70. In the nation: how to help the motorist. Tom Wicker.

*New York Times. p 38. Jl. 29, '70. Too much for highways . . . [editorial].

New York Times. p 1+. S. 30, '70. House approves $10-billion plan for mass transit. Christopher Lydon.

New York Times. p 1+. O. 1, '70. Judge bars order to drop 14 trains. R. E. Bedingfield.

New York Times. p 1+. O. 15, '70. Congress votes company [Railpax] to run passenger trains. Marjorie Hunter.

New York Times. p 40. O. 16, '70. A token for mass transit [editorial].

New York Times. p 82. O. 16, '70. Nixon signs transit bill, terming it a "landmark."

New York Times. p 82. O. 16, '70. Rail route plan due in 30 days for national passenger service [Railpax]. Robert Lindsey.

Newsweek. 66:69-71. Jl. 19, '65. BART. San Francisco's grand design.

*Newsweek. 71:63. Mr. 25, '68. Fighting the freeway.

Newsweek. 72:55-6. Ag. 5, '68. Easing the jam.

Newsweek. 73:57-8. Je. 16, '69. Greasing the wheels: trust fund proposal.

Pittsburgh Business Review. 37:1-6. Ag. '67. Pittsburgh's venture into public transit. Edward Jensen.

Popular Mechanics. 133:80-3+. Je. '70. Plane that makes airfields obsolete: British-built Harrier. K. V. Brown.

Popular Science. 195:51-5+. D. '69. Coming: streamliners without wheels. J. A. Volpe.

Popular Science. 196:86-8. My. '70. Your STOL-bus is coming. Ben Kocivar.

Progressive Architecture. 50:92-115. S. '69. People and planes; can airports bridge the gap? Don Raney.

*Public Interest. no 18 p 52-74. Winter '70. Mass transportation: Cinderella in our cities.

Public Interest. no 18 p 75-87. Winter '70. Transportation and poverty. J. F. Kain and J. R. Meyer.

Railway Age. 163:16-19. O. 2, '67. The airport trains are on the way.

Railway Age. 164:19-20. F. 5, '68. Where is the Federal transit program going? Gordon Allott.

Railway Age. 167:98-9. F. '69. "Busways" may woo the rider back to mass transit. J. C. Corradino.

Railway Age. 167:14-16. N. 3, '69. Hopes rise (again) for a strong transit bill. R. M. Coultas.

Railway Age. 167:16. N. 3, '69. Why Nixon rejected a transit trust fund.

*Railway Age. 167:30-1. D. 15, '69. About those Metroliners: a consultant admits (happily) that he was wrong. W. E. Griswold.

*Railway Age. 168:30-1. Ja. 5/12, '70. TACV: Tomorrow's mass transit vehicle? Philip Harrison.

Railway Age. 168:18-19. F. 2/9, '70. For Mexico's Metro, mañana is today.

Railway Age. 168:20-1. F 2/9, '70. Cities advised: get ready now for transit aid.

Railway Age. 168:22-5. Mr. 9, '70. Is there a better way to get to the airport? David Thaler.

Reporter. 38:21-3. F. 8, '68. Reconciling the conflict of highways and cities. Priscilla Dunhill.

Saturday Evening Post. 241:22-7+. D. 14, '68. American highway: do we know where we're going? R. J. Whalen.

*Saturday Review. 53:31-8+. Ja. 3, '70. Will it be the soaring seventies? Horace Sutton and David Butwin.

Saturday Review. 53:14-17+. Ag. 15, '70. Is the SST necessary? Horace Sutton.

Science News. 94:131-2. Ag. 10, '68. Unjamming the airways.

*Senior Scholastic. 86:6-9. F. 4, '65. The ubiquitous auto . . . man's servant or master?

Time. 92:20. Ag. 2, '68. Saturated sky.

Time. 94:42-3. Ag. 22, '69. Jets v. Everglades.

*Time. 95:48. Ja. 5, '70. The unloved passenger.

*Time. 95:52-6. Ja. 19, '70. Ready or not, here comes Jumbo.

Time. 95:64. Je. 1, '70. SST: boon or boom-doggle?

Time. 96:58-61. Jl. 6, '70. The biggest bankruptcy ever: Penn Central's financial collapse.

Time. 96:59. Jl. 6, '70. The case for—and against—[railroad] nationalization.

Traffic Quarterly. 21:395-405. Jl. '67. High-speed rail passenger transportation and regional development in the Midwest. H. M. Mayer.

Trans-Action. 7:47-54. F. '70. Taxis, jitneys and poverty. Sandi Rosenbloom.

U.S. News & World Report. 62:74-6. My. 15, '67. Breakthrough in mass transit.

U.S. News & World Report. 66:82-4. My. 19, '69. How to move a nation: latest ideas in mass transit.

U.S. News & World Report. 67:66. Ag. 18, '69. Billions for transit; where money will go.

*U.S. News & World Report. 68:58-9. Ja. 19, '70, What's being planned to save rail travel.

U.S. News & World Report. 68:60-1. Ja. 19, '70. Search for the steam-driven car.

*U.S. News & World Report. 68:34-5. Mr. 2, '70. 320 billion dollars more for future highways?

U.S. News & World Report. 68:48-9. My. 25, '70. Untangling big-city traffic: the big push for mass transit.

*Vital Issues. 14 no 6:p 1-4. F. '65. Urban transit. W. S. Rainville, Jr.

Vital Speeches of the Day. 35:279-82. F. 15, '69. Public selects its transportation: address, January 15, 1969. S. E. Knudsen.

Vital Speeches of the Day. 35:657-61. Ag. 15, '69. Decline of rail passenger traffic; the public service obligation of railroads; address, June 19, 1969. G. W. Hilton.

Wall Street Journal. p 32. F. 13, '68. Muted whistle-stops: escalated termination of passenger trains causes woes to hundreds of communities. D. C. Anderson.

Wall Street Journal. p 16. Je. 27, '68. In transit with the road lobbyists. R. A. Buel.

Wall Street Journal. p 1+. F. 4, '70. Cleaner auto fuel: natural gas promoted as freer of pollutants, cheaper than gasoline. J. C. Tanner.

*Wall Street Journal. p 1+. My. 12, '70. Passengers' plaint: more people protest loss of train service, but results are mixed. A. R. Karr.

*Washington Post. p B 6. F. 1, '70. The psychological side of rapid transit. J. E. Clayton.